W9-DEB-893

The String Instrument Owner's Handbook

The String Instrument Owner's Handbook

Michael J. Pagliaro

ROWMAN & LITTLEFIELD
Lanham • Boulder • New York • London

Published by Rowman & Littlefield
A wholly owned subsidiary of The Rowman & Littlefield Publishing Group, Inc.
4501 Forbes Boulevard, Suite 200, Lanham, Maryland 20706
www.rowman.com

Unit A, Whitacre Mews, 26-34 Stannary Street, London SE11 4AB

British Library Cataloguing in Publication Information Available

Library of Congress Cataloging-in-Publication Data
Pagliaro, Michael J.
 The string instrument owner's handbook / Michael J. Pagliaro.
   pages cm
 Includes index.
 ISBN 978-0-8108-8897-5 (cloth : alk. paper) — ISBN 978-0-8108-8898-2 (ebook) 1.
Bowed stringed instruments. 2. Bowed stringed instruments.—Maintenance and repair.
3. Bowed stringed instruments—Construction. I. Title.
 ML750.P34 2015
 787'.192—dc23
                          2015001813

♾ The paper used in this publication meets the minimum requirements of American
National Standard for Information Sciences—Permanence of Paper for Printed Library
Materials, ANSI/NISO Z39.48-1992.

Printed in the United States of America

Contents

Preface

The four instruments of the violin family evolved from the same roots, produce sound in very similar ways, and are structurally alike. They use very similar maintenance procedures, are marketed and rented through the same venues and they are sufficiently similar in their gestalt to warrant sharing a guide.

In the "simplest terms" the viola, cello, and double bass "appear to be" expanded versions of the violin. The operative phrases are "simplest terms" and "appear to be" for, aside from the appearance and the general structure of these instruments, there are some significant historical, acoustical and performing differences. The reader will find in the history chapter it is most likely that the larger instruments preceded the violin. These differences, although significant, do not preclude the possibility a student of one of these instruments could become a student of all of them. Transitioning from one to another is plausible since many but not all playing techniques and music reading skills are transferable.

The String Instrument Owner's Handbook can be read from cover to cover or used as a reference source to directly approach any of the topics listed as chapter headings. The reader can start at any point in this guide to seek a specific bit of information and find the presentation will be as clear as it would be if the content were read starting from the first chapter.

Each chapter begins with a brief overview which serves as an expanded table of contents to assist the reader in pursuing a specific issue. To facilitate that end, references are made to other chapters that contain information relevant to the topic at hand. Moreover, some material from other chapters will be repeated to ease the reader through a concept by avoiding the interruptions necessitated by turning to other chapters.

Acknowledgments

The following individuals have generously contributed their talent and effort to assist in the final production of this work. My most grateful appreciation to:

My son, Michael J. Pagliaro, Jr., for his work in producing and editing the photographs.

My grandson, Michael J. Pagliaro, III, for his drawings and design contributions.

James O'Keefe, artist, sculptor, and computer technology specialist for producing the computerized graphics, drawings of the ancient instruments, fingering charts, and for finessing the formatting and cover of this book.

Thomas Caserta, celebrated academic in the New York area. As a premier S.A.T. test preparation specialist, Tom applied his extensive knowledge of English grammar and usage acquired through his Jesuit education at Fordham Preparatory School and Fordham University to assist in editing the text in this book.

The following extraordinarily gifted professionals in the field of musical instrument fabrication and distribution have generously granted permission to use information and artwork from their websites. Listed in alphabetical order they are:

Bob and Mark Gollihur, double bass authorities at
http://www.gollihurmusic.com;
Scott Hershey, master luthier at
http://www.hersheyviolins.net;
Eitan Hoffer, archetier extraordinaire, specialist in the fabrication of ancient bows at
http://www.hoffer-bows.com;
Lars Kirmser, publisher and musical instrument specialist at
http://www.musictrader.com;
Gregg Miner, President, The Harp Guitar Foundation at
http://www.minermusic.com;
Otis A. Tomas, master luthier at
www.otis@fiddletree.com;

Jimmy Sang Wang, bow manufacturer at http://www.wangbow.com.

Bennett Graff, a special note of appreciation to my editor for the support, encouragement, and technical assistance he has given me in assembling and formatting this manuscript.

Introduction

The String Instrument Owner's Handbook provides a new or experienced owner of an instrument with information that will enhance the ownership experience. This comprehensive treatise includes facts that are relevant to all phases of instrument ownership.

Beginning with a brief history, the guide explains how the instruments work, their variants, how they are made, and who makes them. It then offers guidelines on how to buy and rent one, the care and maintenance needed to keep one, a complete list of the accessories both necessary and desirable, and a glossary of terms both alphabetical and pictorial.

The guide ends with an owner's diary where one can enter the history of an instrument and keep an ongoing record of the service and repairs made over time. Keeping such a diary will not only provide a historical record, but can be a valuable aid in scheduling maintenance procedures that will ensure an instrument's longevity.

The Soul of a String Instrument

The following is an excerpt from a book entitled *The Fiddletree*, written by Otis A. Tomas, a luthier of extraordinary talent. Through his introspection, Otis transmits a sensitivity to string instrument making that transcends the physical act. In so doing, he carries the reader to another dimension of the luthier's art rarely, if ever, communicated by those who describe the process. Tomas writes about a tree which stood on his property for centuries, how he labored with the prospect of cutting it down, and after he did, how he reflected on the act with the following words:

March, 1982

I will remember that day every time I take a chisel to a piece of this wood. I made a promise to myself and to the tree that I will always handle it with care, bringing to it the respect it deserves, and making an effort to use my art to bring new life from old. As the tree lay there on the ground, I stood for a moment and then began to carefully size it up, looking first for the biggest usable pieces — 'cellos and guitars — and working down to the smaller pieces for violins. I noticed the wild figured grain, and watching out for defects, I carefully chunked it into pieces that I could haul out in my arms to the road. This was where I first got a chance to really examine what the tree had to offer.

The deeply figured grain that was predominant in the lower part of the trunk was evidence of the age and character of the old tree. Down by the roots the wood sported some large burls and showed the wildest wrinkling of the grain. A little further up the tree, the radial surfaces showed a strong irregular flaming in the figure, while the slab cuts showed a "quilted" surface, giving the appearance of blisters, bubbles, and clouds.

Higher up the tree, the grain showed itself as strong, straight and even. Once back at the workshop, I further sawed it up into individual pieces, roughly sized for the various instruments. Then I sealed the end grain with wax to prevent it from checking, and carried it upstairs to stack in the loft of my workshop.

Then it was a matter of waiting for time to do its work. It would be several years before I could proceed any further. More than just the drying of the wood, which can be quickly and efficiently accomplished with the careful use of kiln, it is important to let the wood season and age, to let it go through the cycles of humidity and dryness, summer and winter, heat and cold. The effect of proper aging of the wood is something that is hard to measure — unlike moisture content — but I am convinced that just because some things are not measurable, it does not mean that they are insignificant. Many things about the violin are like this — not the least, the effect that its music has upon us.

Stradivari is said to have gotten his wood — all in the hopes of reproducing the fabled sounds of the famous Cremonese masters, as if this were enough to turn us and our creations all into Stradivarius. But per-

haps we don't really need to be constantly searching the far corners of the world for something that we fear we are missing."

Thomas comments later on: *It is the unique and random character of this wood that so strikes me — an unconscious memory and history that is felt so strongly that you can almost read it in the lines of the wood. I feel like I am holding the tree's heart in my hands. This piece of wood will soon become a fiddle and will be joining those other instruments that have already taken shape.*

Chapter 1
Where These Instruments Came From

Introduction

The First String Instruments
The history of musical instruments has been investigated by some of the greatest minds in musicology and academia with results mired in conflicting opinions, contradictory factoids, and a general disarray and confusion of information. Because of this conflict and confusion the following pages dealing with that history are intended to be a simple survey of the subject based on assorted points of view on each topic. In many cases the "experts" themselves qualify their findings with a disclaimer similar to this one.

In an attempt to avoid the endless dialog that would be required to elaborate on these issues, this first section of the survey will cover the history of "non-bowed, plucked or strummed string instruments." The sections which follow will give an overview of what probably happened which resulted in the evolution of the violin family instruments we now use. Timelines preceding each section will show the sequence in which the instruments appeared.

This chapter is divided into four parts. Part 1 will deal with plucked instruments, part 2 with early bowed instruments, part 3 with the appearance of the violin family of instruments, and part 4 will cover the history of the bows.

Plucked Instruments

Timeline
The following timeline shows some of the early plucked instruments in an ethereal, non-specific setting representative of the lack of their exact history. This is the first phase in the evolution of string instruments.

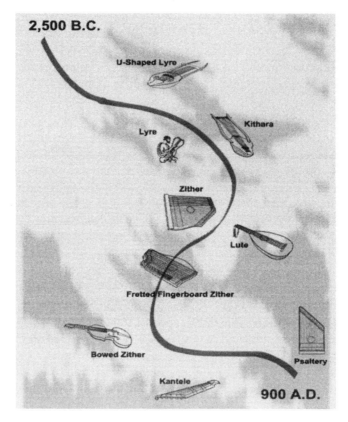

Musical instruments have been in existence in various forms for millennia. One might speculate that several thousand years B.C., someone set a single taut string in motion and it generated a sound. That action would have been the first step in the evolution of string instruments. The three classifications of string instruments that developed from that fundamental experience are those that are played by plucking strings, by strumming more than one string at a time, and by bowing strings.

Plucked string instruments are played by plucking individual strings with the fingers as one does when playing a harp or with a plectrum (pick) on a guitar. A strumming technique, often used when playing a guitar, requires the player to pass the fingers or plectrum across several strings at once. Both of these techniques are interchangeable. The strings on all string instruments can be plucked or strummed.

Bowing is the method used to play the instruments of the violin family, namely, the violin, viola, cello, and double bass. The plucking and strumming techniques can also be used on these instruments but the reverse is not possible on the plucked and strummed instruments because the bodies of those instruments do not provide a place for a bow to pass over the strings effectively.

Evidence of the existence of non-bowed string instruments dates as far back as 2500 B.C. in Mesopotamia (Iraq). Among the instruments that existed prior to the appearance of those of the violin family were lyres, lutes, zithers, kanteles, and psalteries. These plucked string instruments were primarily used as accompaniment for vocal solos and oral presentations of poetry and prose.

The Lyre

The term *lyre* is applied to a wide spectrum of instruments with strings. Dictionary definitions of lyre range from a "*U*" shaped instrument with strings which are plucked to a category of early medieval bowed instruments. The consistency of inconsistency often rears its ugly head in matters of the music world.

The early instruments that fall into the "*U*" shaped plucked lyre category had a basic structure consisting of a hollow base at the bottom of the instrument which acted as a resonating chamber. Two arms, one attached on either side of the chamber were connected at the top by a bar which served as a structural support for the instrument.

The strings, usually gut, were attached to the top connecting bar, extended down over a bridge and were attached at the bottom resonating chamber. In some instruments the strings were connected directly to the bridge whereas on others the strings went over the bridge, continuing on to a tailpiece (Fig. 1.1).

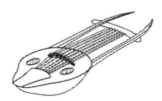

Figure 1.1 "*U*" Shaped Lyre

The different pitches of the strings of the "*U*" shaped lyre were achieved by increased thickness for the lower notes or by adjusting the strings' tension. This basic lyre structure appeared to be the foundation for the myriad versions of plucked string instruments that appeared in ancient Persia, Greece, and Rome. Some of these instruments eventually became the Spanish guitar. Illustrations from various art forms show seven-string instruments being held with the left hand and plucked with the right hand (Fig. 1.2).

Figure 1.2 Seven-String Plucked Instrument

Other later examples show similar instruments with as few as four and as many as ten strings. Since very few actual instruments have survived or have been discovered thus far, conclusions regarding their design and the manner in which they were played continue to be based on speculation and observations of the artwork from the period under study.

The Kithara

The kithara is one of the early instruments that meets the requirements needed to be included in the lyre category because it had the basic lyre structure of a resonating chamber, side arms and strings attached to a

cross bar on top. The kithara pictured in Figure 1.3 shows the strings passing over a bridge and attached to a violin-like tailpiece as opposed to being attached directly to the instrument's base. The player used a plectrum to pluck the strings. The kithara was used as an accompaniment to recitations of prose, poetry, vocal performances, and dancing.

Figure 1.3 Kithara

The Lute

The lute differs from the "U" shaped lyre category of instruments in that its basic structure is similar to that of the violin with some variants and with an entirely different appearance. Starting at the top, the lute has a peg box with tuning pegs to which strings are connected. The peg box in earlier lutes was bent back at a significant angle (Fig. 1.4).

Figure 1.4 Lute

The peg box was followed by a nut, a fretted fingerboard, and a bridge to which the gut strings were directly attached. The frets were made by tying gut around the fingerboard. Wooden frets were sometimes strategically located to aid in shifting registers as would a capo on a guitar.

The body of the lute was pear-shaped with the back built of wooden strips as opposed to the violin back which is either one piece or two at most. The top of the lute was made of one piece but with only one tone hole called a rose in the center of the top.

Among musical instrument historians (organologists), there is disagreement as to whether a long-necked lute appearing significantly earlier than the short-necked lute disqualifies the former from holding a position in the lute family

The Zither

Zither is a label applied to string instruments that share a structure where all the strings are extended across a sound board. They were designed to be played on a flat surface or on the player's lap, varied greatly in size and shape but generally took the form of an elongated hollow box. Zithers could range in size anywhere from approximately a square foot up to three square feet.

Unlike more contemporary instruments such as the violin or guitar, the variety of shapes and sizes of instruments called zithers which have evolved throughout the centuries is so remarkably abundant and wracked with conflicting data and opinion that it is not possible to chronicle this instrument's evolution in one section of one chapter. Some attribute the popularity of these instruments to their acoustic simplicity since constructing one originally required little more than basic cabinetmaker skills and a musical inclination.

This category of instrument can be found built with three configurations. In one arrangement the instrument does not have a neck or frets so there is no opportunity for the player to adjust the pitch while playing a given string. The strings can be plucked or strummed like those of the guitar but each string can produce only the pitch to which it is tuned (Fig. 1.5).

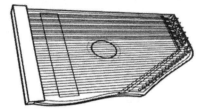

Figure 1.5 The Zither

In another design there is a fretted fingerboard with about five strings that run parallel to the soundboard. These strings are used to play the melody while the remaining strings can be strummed or plucked as accompanying figures (Fig 1.6).

Figure 1.6 The Fretted Fingerboard Zither

The bowed zither deviates from the common box-shaped instrument to provide a structure where a bow can pass over strings. This modification was accomplished by changing the shape of the sounding body to either a triangle, violin shape, or some other configuration that would allow a bow to pass over the strings (Fig. 1.7)

Figure 1.7 The Bowed Zither

A significant contribution to understanding the history of plucked instruments by clarifying this array of scattered information is the Fretless Zither Family Tree (Fig. 1.8) created by Gregg Miner and Kelly Williams. Mr. Miner notes that the "evolution" tree line that reads "inspired" means that those two separate historical instrument lines *may* have inspired the first or later inventors of the endless number of fretless zithers.

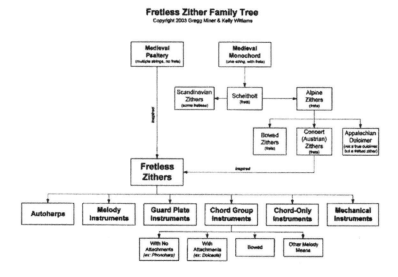

Figure 1.8 The Fretless Zither Family Tree
(Reproduced with permission of Gregg Miner.)

The Kantele

The kantele is considered to be one of the earliest of the plucked zither family instruments. Its origins date back several thousand years to the Baltic countries where references to the instrument can be found in Finnish literature of that period. Following the pattern of its cousins, the kantele was not used as a solo instrument but rather as an accompaniment to prose and vocal performances.

By virtue of its design and prescribed playing technique, the kantele falls into the category of the zither family. The instrument had a hollow wooden body which acted as a sound resonator over which five horsehair or gut strings were stretched. They were joined to tuning pins at one end and at the other end to a crossbar. The absence of a bridge or nut resulted in a distinctive bell-like sound associated with that instrument (Fig. 1.9).

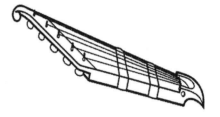

Figure 1.9 The Kantele

The strings were tuned to either a major or minor diatonic scale. The kantele was placed on a flat surface or on the player's lap where it could be strummed or plucked with the fingers or a plectrum. When played with the fingers, it was possible to produce both melody and accompaniment by judiciously assigning each finger to a particular string. Most music played on the early kantele was improvised rather than prescribed.

The Psaltery

The psaltery is another version of zither with a series of pre-tuned strings attached at the top and bottom of a soundboard. The pitch for each string was a product of its length; therefore, higher- pitched strings were shorter and lower pitches were longer. To accommodate this arrangement, the sounding board body of the psaltery had to assume a trapezoidal shape (Fig. 1.10).

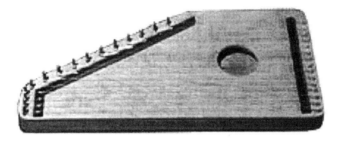

Figure 1.10 The Psaltery

At some point it became apparent that a sound produced by rubbing a tacky stick or chord across a string would produce a sustained richer sound than that produced by plucking the string. And so appeared the bowed psaltery. This triangle-shaped instrument was developed with a string pattern that would facilitate the process of a bow being applied to one string at a time (Fig. 1.11).

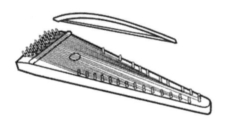

Figure 1.11 The Bowed Psaltery

Summary

Among the early images of non-bowed string instruments is ornamentation on a sarcophagus in Crete dated 1400 B.C. Numerous other examples are to be found in all forms of art throughout the centuries to follow. The wide variety of shapes and iterations seen in these illustrations can be thought-provoking while confusing since it becomes difficult to separate accuracy and fact from artistic license and imagination. One must wonder how much of what is evidenced in art from the past actually did exist.

The number and variety of plucked and strummed string instruments that preceded the appearance of the first bowed string instruments are as great and diverse as to make documenting their evolution with any degree of accuracy almost impossible. The most dedicated organologists can, at best, compile a treatise on the instruments from those millennia based mostly on speculation and deduction.

Early Bowed Instruments

The following timeline shows the second phase in the evolution of string instruments. The exact timeline of this period continues to be somewhat vague but there is a bit more specificity by virtue of increased secondary sources from which one can make reasonable assumptions with respect as to how the instruments continued to evolve.

This period also shares the same dearth of specific documentation concerning its history. The absence of facts continued up to the beginning of the sixteenth century, when the history of musical instruments began to be recorded. Prior to that point, one had to rely on literature and poetry on other subjects that contained references to string instruments because few actual early instruments have survived. The texts from these writings indicate that instruments with strings that were both bowed and plucked did exist. More graphic examples are found in the paintings and statues from the early centuries showing the instruments being played.

Numerous music-producing devices with a body of some sort, either containing a fingerboard or connected to a type of fingerboard with a peg box and strung with tunable strings, began to appear at about 900 A.D. These instruments functioned in a manner similar to that of modern non-fretted string instruments and so might logically be considered to be their predecessors. However, the evidence is scattered and lacking in valid source material and so it is not possible to trace the "invention" of the instruments of the violin family back to a particular point in time. Among the most likely precursors of the viola and violin were, respectively, the rebab, rebec, vielle, viola da braccio, and viola da gamba. The cello and double bass then followed as an outgrowth of the viola and violin.

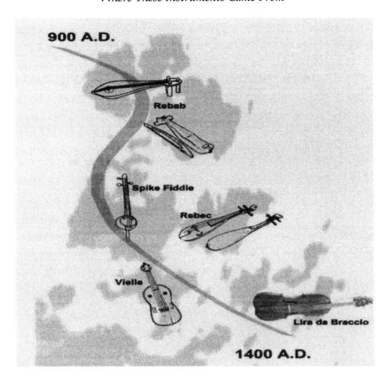

The Rebab

The Arabic word *rebab* refers to a bowed string instrument. The rebab was usually constructed with a pear-shaped body that was hollowed out from a block of wood. A thin sheet of wood or animal hide was then attached to the hollowed-out section to act as a top. Unlike the modern violin, the fingerboard was constructed as part of the body instead of as separate piece attached to the instrument (Fig. 1.12).

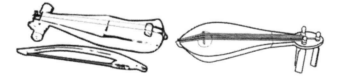

Figure 1.12 The Rebab

Rebabs are generally thought to have had two strings, though one will find references to some models with three strings. The rebab was played with a bow and was used both as a solo instrument and as accompaniment to dialog and singing. As far back as the eighth century, the rebab was being played in North Africa, the Middle East, and in Europe. Its widespread popularity can be attributed to the simplicity of design, portability, and playability. Rebabs circulated throughout the Islamic trade routes of the time.

The Spike Fiddle

Another form of rebab, a spike fiddle, was constructed with a round body. The neck on this instrument supported the strings and consisted of a rounded pole which extended down through the body to form an endpin. The player held the spike fiddle upright, resting it on the ground or on the player's lap (Fig. 1.13).

Figure 1.13 The Spike Fiddle

The Rebec

The rebec, which has a body, fingerboard, and tuning pegs similar to those of the rebab, may be an expansion of that instrument (Fig. 1.14). A significant difference between the two is found in the body of the rebec which was carved from a solid piece of wood as opposed to being created from a gourd or fabricated gourd shape. The body of the rebec was boat shaped, and the fingerboard with its tuning pegs was a separate entity attached to the body as compared to the rebab fingerboard being part of the body.

The rebec originally had two strings similar to the rebab with a third string being added later on. The rebec enjoyed its popularity in Europe during the fifteenth and sixteenth centuries.

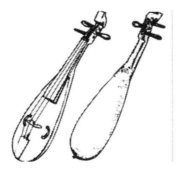

Figure 1.14 The Rebec

The Vielle

The Vielle appeared somewhat earlier in France during the medieval period from the thirteenth to the fifteenth century (Fig. 1.15). This instrument was closer in design to the modern violin. Rather than having a gourd-shaped body, as did the rebab and rebec, the vielle's body was constructed with an upper and lower bout shape and a narrower mid-section which allowed a player to use a bow more easily.

Figure 1.15 The Vielle

The body of the vielle was larger than that of the modern violin in both length and depth and had a flat peg box with the pegs protruding from the top. The vielle had five strings as compared to the two and three strings of the rebab and the rebec, respectively, and was most popularly used by troubadours who were writers of poetry and music of the period. The vielle found its way into all levels of society from the intellectual elite to the common man. Currently, attempts to recreate these instruments from the thirteenth and fourteenth centuries are under way by luthiers who are taking their clues from stone carvings and ancient paintings.

The Beginning of the Violin Family

The Lira da Braccio

N.B. One will find reference to this instrument as lira da braccio, di braccio, and da braccia. Correct Italian grammar would dictate that the word *braccio* be preceded by the preposition *di*, or *braccia*, by *da*. This is just one example of the inconsistencies one will come across in researching the history of instruments of the violin family.

Following the vielle in the evolution of bowed string instruments was the lira da braccio or di braccio (of the arm) which first appeared in Italy. This was a bowed string instrument more closely resembling a violin but with a wider fingerboard. (Fig. 1.16)

Figure 1.16 Lira da Braccio
(Kunsthistorisches Museum, Musikinstrumente, Vienna, Austria)

The lira da braccio could have as many as seven strings. Four were tuned to E, A, D, and G over a fingerboard as are those of a violin. An additional low D string was also placed over the fingerboard, and two other strings ran parallel to as opposed to over the fingerboard. These two strings tuned in octaves were played as drones or pedal tones. The tuning pegs on the lira da braccio were installed on the top of a leaf-shaped peg box instead of on the sides as on contemporary instruments.

Scholars have deduced that the upper strings of the lira da braccio were used to play the melody while chords using triple and quadruple stops were played on the lower strings. The technique needed to play this combination of tones simultaneously limited the performer in both versatility and in the use of harmonic inversions. These limitations led performers to migrate eventually toward the Andrea Amati violin for its sweet sound and for all of the versatility that we know is possible when a violin is played by a well-trained musician.

Considering all of the history outlined above, one may conclude that the instruments we know today are more a culmination of a multi-century evolution of plucked and bowed stringed instruments than actual inventions. It is not possible to name an "inventor" of the violin as we know it today; however, the two names that appear as most likely candidates for the title are Andrea Amati and Gasparo da Salo. It was during their productive years that recorded history began to appear. The records documented to some degree the biographies and instruments of prominent luthiers of the time.

An in-depth look at the records from that period will show a growing number of luthiers from every part of Europe. These artisans advanced the development of the four string instruments of the violin family in many directions. Unfortunately, the problem becomes not one of insufficient documentation but rather of a tsunami of somewhat loosely connected anecdotal evidence describing the works of all these individuals, their biographies, and their contributions. Supporting that written history are some of the actual instruments still in existence that were made by those luthiers. What better original source material can a music historian ask for?

The First Violin?

Gasparo di Bertolotti da Salo (Gasparo da Salo) of Brescia (C.1540-1609) and Andrea Amati of Cremona (C.1525-1611) were luthiers who are considered to be makers of the first violin. There is some confusion with respect to who holds that title because the records show that Amati was known as a "lute maker" as opposed to a "violin maker." Those on the Amati side justify his position by saying that the term violin was still in its infancy, not known to many and, therefore, not applied to Amati. There are recorded documents showing that Amati sold 24 violins to Charles IX of France in 1560. Fourteen of these are still in existence. On the basis of that fact, one could then justifiably conclude that Amati was, indeed, a violin maker. What is generally accepted is that both men made significant contributions to the original design of the violin we use today.

The evolution of musical instrument technology and an increasing demand by contemporary composers for more versatility and tone projection from string instruments has prompted some changes to be made to the neck, fingerboard, sound post, and bass bar of the existing so-called "Baroque" or original instruments of the sixteenth and seventeenth centuries. The higher tension strings that were developed in later years to increase volume and improve tone production required the instruments to have a longer neck with a slightly elevated angle of projection of the fingerboard. This change also called for a heavier bass bar and sound post to conduct that additional sound throughout the instrument. (See chapter 3 on Baroque violins.) As a result, most, if not all surviving instruments from that period have been subjected to those changes.

The Schools

The word *school* will most often bring to mind a structure in which groups of children and others receive some form of education. A lesser-known definition refers to a location consisting of a broader geographic area where, over a period of time, a group of individuals with a common interest live and work in close proximity. Their goal was to develop their skills and broaden their knowledge to advance their cause. Such was the case with luthiers from the mid-fifteen hundreds to about 1725. During that period, the violin, viola, cello, and double bass were developed and refined to the extraordinarily high degree of perfection we enjoy today.

Over a period of some 200 years, a number of such schools began to appear throughout Europe. Among them were the Brescian, Cremonese, Neapolitan, Tyrolean, and French schools. Each is named for the geographic location where it was centered and where its inhabitants distinguished themselves by making significant contributions to the development of the instruments of the violin family.

Timeline

The time periods during which the "Schools" were active is estimated on the basis of the participating luthiers' productive lives.

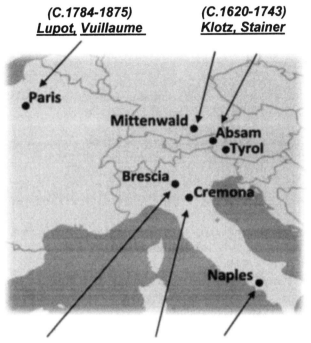

(C.1784-1875)
Lupot, Vuillaume

(C.1620-1743)
Klotz, Stainer

Gasparo da Salo
Maggini, Rogeri
(C.1585-1895)

Amati, Bergonzi,* Gagliano,*
Guarneri, Ruggieri, Stradivari
(C. 1541-1744)
*Bergonzi & Gagliano worked in Cremona and Naples

Cremonese School

Andrea Amati (1525-1611) was the principal figure in the Cremonese school of violin making. His early works consisted of rebecs and other string instruments that preceded the violin. At this point in time, historians begin to see actual documentation showing the development of the instruments of the string family. Amati and his contemporaries were commissioned by royalty (King Charles IX of France) and wealthy aristocrats such as the Medici family to make a variety of instruments for use in the courts and at lavish gatherings. During this period the violin began to take hold as the instrument of choice and consequently the art of making string instruments began to flourish.

The Amati family consisted of Andrea, Antonio, Girolamo, Nicolo, and Girolamo II, all of whom carried on the Amati tradition of making extraordinary string instruments up to 1740. Their gift to the music world endures in their instruments that have survived along with the improvements and innovations they made that are still in use today.

Nicolo, Andrea's grandson, is considered by many to have produced the finest of the Amati instruments. He served as teacher to many of the master luthiers of that period. Amati's sons, Gerolamo, Antonio, and Nicolo, and Andrea's nephews, devoted some of their luthier skills to the development of the double bass. Unfortunately, interest in this large instrument waned because of its size and the amount of wood and labor needed to produce one. Other contemporaries of the Amati family were Jacob Stainer, later to join the Tyrolean School, Antonio Stradivari and his two sons, Francesco and Omobono, and the five members of the Guarneri family including Andrea, Pietro, Giuseppe, Giuseppe del Gesu, and Pietro de Venice.

Antonio Stradivari (1644-1737) was independently wealthy allowing him the liberty to experiment and develop his craftsmanship as he wished. It is believed that he worked as an apprentice in the Nicolo Amati shop. However, some doubt about that fact is raised by the lack of Stradivari-signed works from that period, which is another bit of information one might put into the "early luthier mysteries" file.

Stradivari's productive life, which was, in fact, almost every day of his life, can be divided into three periods. The first period was the Amati period from 1668 to 1686, where his instruments manifested the Amati pattern with some modifications. This period was followed by a span of about eight years where Stradivari's longer and narrower instruments took on a more sophisticated elegance. During these years he developed a different, lighter varnish evident on those instruments. It was not until his last period from 1695 on to the end of his life that Stradivari's instruments reached the magnificence of tone production and physical perfection for which he has been lauded for centuries. Some suggest that the instruments he made after 1725, when he was in his eighties, show a decline in workmanship. In his lifetime Antonio Stradivari made upward of one thousand instruments.

Francesco Ruggieri (1620-1695) is said to have been Nicolo Amati's first pupil. After a shorter than usual apprenticeship, Ruggieri proceeded on his own to make violins in the pattern he learned under the Amati family. Ruggieri is recognized for developing a more refined pattern for the cello. This instrument was very well received for its smaller size which became a model for future cello makers.

Carlo Bergonzi (1683-1747), also from the Cremonese school, ranks in skill as a luthier just a shade below Stradivari. A neighbor and then student of Stradivari, Bergonzi was able to refine his talents as a violin maker to the point where he became Stradivari's repair technician. Bergonzi was so highly regarded in this role that his repair business prevented him from making many violins. His luthier skills are most admired for the extraordinary degree of perfection and the balance of form he was able to achieve in the construction of his instruments. Most notable was the perfectly symmetrical elegance of his scrolls.

Brescian School

Located in the Lombardy region of northern Italy, Brescia, the second largest city in that region, is situated at the base of the Alps. In the period between 1585 and 1895, Brescia became a center for master luthiers. In this luthier's mecca, the violin, viola, cello, and double bass were conceived and developed from their predecessors, the viola da braccia, viola da gamba, and the many other viols that had evolved up to that time. These older instruments served as models from which the luthiers developed the four instruments of the violin family. This is not to say that the process was premeditated or by design. Rather, it was a natural outgrowth of the need to provide musicians with instruments that would cover the soprano, alto, tenor, and bass range of the human voice. One can also find in the documented history of Brescia the first reference to the term violin (violino), the diminutive of viola.

The two best known names from the Brescian school are Gasparo di Bertolotti, AKA Gasparo da Salo (1542-1609) and Giovanni Maggini (1580-1630). These two master luthiers contributed significantly to the music world with their individualism and experimental creativity. Gasparo di Bertolotti was born in Salo, a town in Italy, and so came the name Gasparo da Salo. During his tenure he developed the longer shape violin that produced the more strident sound needed to hold a position in the brass-oriented ensembles of that time. This elongated shape was to be the model Stradivari used for his instruments.

Da Salo was prolific in his output, not only in his violin making but also in producing different size violins and violas which were intended to play in the alto and tenor range. These included violas da gamba, cellos, double basses and other assorted, lesser known instruments of the string family of that period. The luthiers of the Brescian school were held in highest esteem until the onset of the plague which decimated that population.

A contemporary of da Salo was Giovanni Paolo Maggini (1580-1630). Born in nearby Botticino, Maggini studied at a young age as an apprentice with da Salo and remained in that position until his early twenties. Contrary to his master's violin designs, Maggini developed a pattern featuring a larger configuration with larger sound holes and a lower arching top. His earlier works are considered by some to lack the finesse of those made by the other masters of that time; however, his proclivity to experiment with sound production ultimately resulted in instruments of outstanding quality in the materials they contain, the high degree of artistry in ornamentation, and in the mellifluous sound they produce. He made about seventy-five instruments, mostly violins and violas, two cellos, and what might possibly be one of the first double basses.

Neapolitan School

The Cremonese school of violin making began to diminish in importance as a result of the decline in the economy, the plague, and many years of war and political strife. Concurrently, in the south of Italy, the area of Naples was growing economically and culturally. That expansion fostered an increasing demand for musical instruments which resulted in the growth of the Neapolitan School of violin making. It was in that area from the late 1600s for a period of about one hundred twenty years that a new crop of master luthiers came together geographically and professionally to produce a series of extraordinary instruments.

Alessandro Gagliano (1640-1725) was the head of a family of luthiers that over a period of almost three hundred years provided a direct line from the Cremonese school up to the twentieth century. The Gagliano family closed shop in 1925. Born to an aristocratic family, Alessandro had little formal training developing his skills as a luthier independently. As a result, his workmanship lacked the finesse of his contemporaries but he did distinguish himself with his cellos. These were regarded by many as being distinctive in both design and tone production. He is also lauded for the varnish he developed, which showed new clarity and depth, with a distinctive crimson hue. It is generally accepted by the *cognoscenti* that his varnish is equal to if not better than that of the Cremonese masters.

Unlike Alessandro, his sons and brothers chose to follow the elongated pattern for instruments established by Stradivari. This change then became the norm for most instruments made by luthiers of the Neapolitan school. Alessandro's sons, Nicolo and Gennaro, are considered to have produced the best work of the entire Gagliano family.

Tyrolean School

Parallel in time with the above masters was the Tyrolean School where Jacob Stainer (1620-1683) reigned as prime luthier. Stainer, a student of Nicolaus Amati, developed a somewhat different design for his instruments which featured a much higher arch on the top and back than those of the Stradivari models. Stainer was also noted for his unique scrolls which often featured carved heads in place of the traditional scroll shape.

A contemporary of Stainer was Matthias Klotz (1656-1743). Klotz studied with Stainer and Giovanni Railich in Padua, Italy. The results were instruments that contained the characteristics of both of these masters. Klotz finally settled in Mittenwald, Germany where he used his entrepreneurial skills to develop a complete violin industry. Like the Gagliano family, Klotz's business also became the family business, producing many instruments which are still available today.

French School

Nicholas Lupot (1784-1824) studied under his father, Francois. Nicholas reached his prime by his mid-twenties and was most noted for copying the Stradivari design as well as designs of other masters. Nicolas did not distinguish himself so much for his originality but rather for the delicate refinement he added to the patterns of others. He was ranked by many as the master luthier of the French school.

Keeping with the concept of copying the work of others rather than trying to create his own distinct pattern was Jean-Baptiste Vuillaume (1798-1875). He is to this day still recognized as being able to recreate the styles and varnishes of the master luthiers of the past with extraordinary accuracy. His copies of Stradivari violins were so perfect that some of the current appraisers are still unsure when they attempt to identify a Stradivari instrument if, in fact, it may have been one of the copies made by Vuillaume. Jean-Baptiste was also an entrepreneur. In 1828 he started his own business where he marketed his reproductions along with other high quality instruments. He expanded his business by employing other craftsmen to make bows, resulting in the growth of some of the finest French bow makers of that period.

Summary

The "Schools" of violin making mentioned above are but some of many that came into being throughout Europe beginning in the sixteenth century. Venice and Absam (Austria) along with other lesser known clusters of luthiers on every level served as embryos which gave birth to an entire family of musical instruments that have served and will continue to serve humanity for centuries to come.

The History of Bows

The concept of generating vibrations by rubbing something against a string or some form of idiophone was the exercise that probably resulted in the very earliest bow being created. That "something" could have been some sort of reed or stick with a surface rough enough to generate vibrations. Evidence of cords and hair tied or connected in various ways to bow-shaped sticks appears in drawings dating as far back as the eighth century. That configuration would allow the cords or hairs to have free contact with a string on an instrument and, when rubbed against the string, produce a vibration (sound). Drawings of bows can be found with every conceivable arc shape imaginable. The only reoccurring theme is that they were all designed with a curve to the stick that would accommodate some form of cord-like material or hair.

The lack of source information available to document the early history of instruments of the violin family is even greater for the bows used to play those instruments. A study of sculpture and paintings from the past gives some hint as to the size, shape, structure, and playing positions of the instruments from a given period, but those same artworks give short shrift to the bow. One might speculate that the artists either did not know the important role bows had in sound production or that in the totality of the art work, the bow was in their minds not significant enough to warrant detailed attention.

Those who write on this subject will justifiably hedge on the time of the appearance of the first bows, often referring to the tenth century in central Asia as a starting point where bowed string instruments began to appear. That time frame is one of speculation and not necessarily fact. One begins to see a shape closer to that of the modern bow in the drawings that were made in the seventeenth century. Unfortunately, there is no indication of the exact date when these drawings were made so they cannot be used by musical instrument historians to deduce the sequence of bow development. It is therefore possible that a more sophisticated iteration could have preceded the rendering of a less advanced model.

Beginning in the early Baroque period, a variety of bow designs began to appear as a result of the requirements of a changing style of music composition. Before the appearance of the violin, string instruments were primarily used as backgrounds to musical themes. Consequently, their contribution to an ensemble consisted primarily of rhythmic patterns rather than of melody. Producing rhythmic patterns required a less sophisticated bow and as a result the bows were shorter and had a wider arc designed for the player to use with an underhanded grip.

There are some contemporary bow makers who specialize in making bows in the patterns used in ancient times. The work of these archetiers is the best source for examples and information on this part of musical instrument history. The following are photographs of a few of the many ancient bows made by the contemporary master archetier Eitan Hoffer who operates a shop in Israel. There he makes bows to satisfy the needs of musicians who perform ancient music using period instruments. Below are some pictures of Mr. Hoffer's bows which illustrate the shapes that preceded those of the contemporary bows we now use. The following examples of ancient bows were reproduced with permission of Eitan Hoffer, Bow Maker (www.hoffer-bows. com).

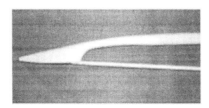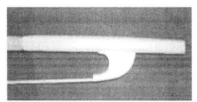

Figure 1.17 Renaissance Viol Bow
Made from Yew Wood.

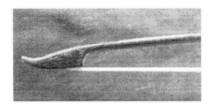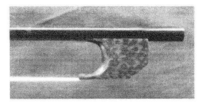

Figure 1.18 Short Violin Bow
Used for late Renaissance and early seventeenth century music, this bow was inspired by an original Italian bow produced at the end of the sixteenth century.

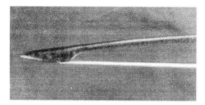
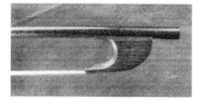

Figure 1.19 Seventeenth Century Style Violin Bow
Made from snake wood, this bow is 66 cm long. The design is based on
paintings where a short, thin bow with a low head (tip) is clearly illustrated.

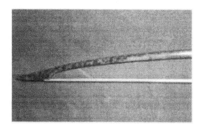
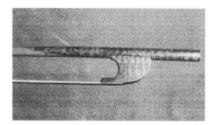

Figure 1.20 Seventeenth Century Short Bow
Based on an original bow (c. 1680), this reproduction is 58 cm long and weighs 40
gr. Note the difference in size of the frog as compared to Figure 1.19.

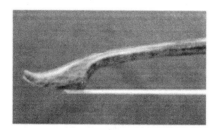
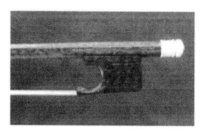

Figure 1.21 French Eighteenth Century Violin Bow With Screw Mechanism.
Made from snake wood with snake wood frog and mammoth ivory button.
One of the early examples of a movable frog.

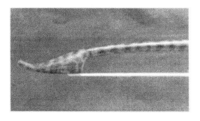
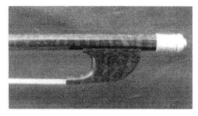

Figure 1.22 Violin "Long Sonata Bow" (C. 1720)
[See previous page] A reproduction of the original bow in the Ashmolean museum in Oxford (Hill collection no. 19) which was ideal for playing early eighteenth century music like that of Corelli, Vivaldi, and J.S. Bach.

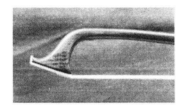

Figure 1.23 Classical Bow
Based on an Original Bow by N. Duchaine (c. 1765).

In mid-seventeenth century Italy the music began to emphasize a lyrical, bel canto style which motivated the Italian musicians to gravitate toward using the more flexible, graceful overhand bow grip. This hand position, in conjunction with a longer, better balanced bow, facilitated the player's greater control. With that control came an expansion of bowing techniques needed to execute all of the stylistic techniques ranging from a very smooth sensitive tone production to the crisp articulation associated with spiccato bowing. The sticks became straighter, and tended toward the present day camber. The bows became lighter and better balanced and the mechanism to control the tension of the hair more refined.

It was during this period that an extensive variety of bows was produced with different designs that provided the tools for experimentation. This process eventually led to the classic model now known to the music world. The operative word here is "eventually," for there would be yet another period of bow making during which experimentation driven by musical needs continued to drive makers to further perfect their product.

Composers were widening their musical horizons to include a broader spectrum of solo and larger ensemble music. Expanding the instrumentation and intensity of the music gave rise to a myriad of bowing techniques needed to satisfy those musical goals. This, in turn, motivated the bow makers to further refine their products. It was at that time that the metal underslide was added to the space between the frog and the stick, and the tip and frog began to take on the characteristics that are familiar to us today.

During this period a man considered to be the Stradivari of bow making, François Xavier Tourte (1747-1835) began his training as a luthier with his father, Nicolas Pierre (1700-1765). In addition to carrying out his duties as a luthier, Tourte began the improvement of the bow. After his father's demise, Tourte joined with G. B. Viotti, a violin virtuoso, in a successful effort to improve the design of the bow by restructuring the balance, increasing the weight of the frog and tip, and altering the bow's length. (For a detailed view of these bow parts see Figure 2.4 in chapter 2.) Tourte refined the process for creating the camber in the bow stick by using heat instead of the carving method commonly used at the time. Of profound significance was the invention of the moveable frog through the use of the screw and eye mechanism which is currently in use on virtually every bow made today.

In addition to these inventions and improvements was Tourte's innovation to spread the hairs at the frog through the use of a wedge of wood inserted between the hair and the ferrule. As currently seen in bows, this small but very important addition resulted in the individual hairs' being firmly held parallel to one another rather than clumping.

Tourte's obsession with perfection resulted in his destroying any bow made in his shop which in his judgment was not perfect. One might speculate that although this level of perfection resulted in the magnificent bows we all know, this behavior also was responsible for the possible loss of some extraordinary bows which, although not in his eyes perfect enough to enjoy life, would probably serve the music community as splendid tools for the trade. His bow design became the archetype for all the prominent bow makers to follow.

Tourte's redesigning of the balance and structure of the bow stick, along with his mechanical innovations with the frog, not only improved the bow as a tool but also actually changed the sound of the instruments on which these bows are used. The bow on any string instrument is a significant partner in the sound-producing elements not only in terms of the physics of the sound but also as the primary tool the performer has to play the instrument. With the exception of pizzicato (plucked) playing, the player controls every nuance of every note played through the use of the bow. Dynamics, timbre, articulation, volume, phrasing, and all the subtleties of sound production are the result of a partnership among the bow, the player, and the instrument. Because of this confluence, one might safely say Tourte's contributions to bow design revolutionized the acoustics of all bowed string instruments.

The three most renowned bow makers to follow Tourte were Ludwig Bausch (1805-1871), Francois Voirin (1833-1885), and Eugene Sartory (1871-1946). These names are frequently found on contemporary bows just as one can find the name Stradivari on labels of violins not made by him. Such labels are more an indication of style than of origin.

Summary

In response to the original question, "Where did the instruments of the violin family come from?" the short answer must be that there were too many people in too many places doing too many things over too many years to allow any kind of definitive comprehensive statement that could be considered valid. The rebab, rebec, vielle, viola da gamba, and viola da braccia, along with all of the secondary experimental instruments that came and went over the centuries, paved the way for luthiers to settle on the violin, viola, cello, and double bass. These four instruments were most suitable to satisfy the musical needs of performers by providing a complete range of pitches with timbres that were both harmonious and complementary to each other. These basic instrument designs also permitted a performer to exercise technique and musicianship with reasonable facility.

A safe assumption would be that the viola came first, was refined into a violin, expanded into a cello, and then grew into a double bass. When did this happen and who did it? This author has yet to find any specific history that is not modified by some other specific history that tells the story in a slightly different way. The bottom line has to be that many people developed these instruments over a long period of time in different places using original ideas in many different ways. The good news is that we now have all four of these wonderful instruments that will be available to enjoy for centuries to come.

Chapter 2
How These Instruments Work

The four instruments of the violin family, the violin, viola, cello and double bass (Fig. 2.1), are very similar in their design, acoustics, and construction and share many playing techniques and fingering patterns. Understanding the relationship of an instrument to other instruments in the same family eases the transition from individual study to ensemble playing. A knowledge of how an instrument works also significantly facilitates learning how to play it.

Figure 2.1 Violin Family Instruments

Because all the instruments in the violin family work in a similar manner, the violin will be used as the model to describe the process. Figure 2.2 will be used as a model to explain how the four instruments in the family work.

When a string (1) is set into motion, its vibration is conducted by the bridge (2) to the top of the instrument (3), transferred via the sound post (4) to the back (5) and distributed laterally throughout the top by the bass bar (6). The top and back of an instrument are supported by its sides (7). The combined motion of these parts sets the air contained within the body of the instrument into a pumping motion that forces the resonating sound out of the instrument through the "f" holes (8). The purfling (9) controls the vibration of sound throughout the top and back while reinforcing the structure of those two parts of the instrument.

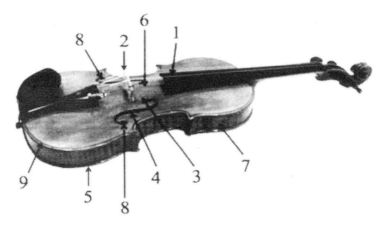

Figure 2.2 Instrument Parts

The Bow

Violin, viola, cello and double bass bows are also very similar in design, construction, and use patterns (Fig. 2.3). The differences are in their size and in the shape of their frogs. The violin frog (A) is squared off at the back. The viola bow (B) is slightly larger in all dimensions and has a rounded edge on the back of the frog. The cello bow (C) is still larger than the viola bow in all dimensions and also has a rounded edge on the back of the frog.

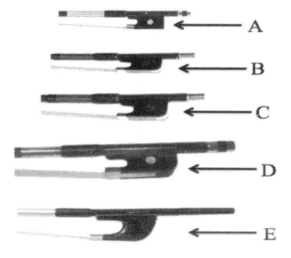

Figure 2.3 Bows

The double bass uses two different types of bows: the French style and the German style. The French bass bow (D) has the same design as that of the viola and cello but is much larger than either. The German bass bow (E) sports a grip-type frog and is held in the palm of the hand with the fingers on the top, side and bottom of the frog. A more detailed description of how these bows are held will follow under the heading sound production.

A bow made of Pernambuco wood and strung with horsehair is the bow of choice. A more cost effective and practical choice for beginning students is a bow made with a fiberglass stick and fiberglass hair or, if possible, horsehair. The fiberglass bows are much less expensive, very durable, and are considered by most teachers of beginning students to be a very adequate substitute for the more expensive wood/horsehair combination. Figure 2.4 is a diagram showing how the hair is installed on a bow.

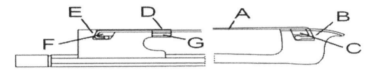

Figure 2.4 Bow Parts

A hank of horse hair (A) is selected and combed so that all hairs are parallel to one another. The end of the hank is then tied and wedged securely into a box-shaped cutout (mortise) at the tip of the bow (B). The hair is held in place by a wooden, wedge-shaped plug (C) that is accurately cut to exactly fit the space remaining in the cutout box.

A metal band called a ferrule (D) is inserted over the hair which is carefully drawn along the bow, tied at the end, and inserted into another box-shaped cutout in the frog (E). A wooden wedge-shaped plug is placed into the box (F) to secure the hair in place. Finally, a slide and third wooden wedge are inserted between the ferrule and the frog (G) to help distribute the hairs equally and laterally and to keep them in place. For more detailed information on this topic see chapter 4 on how bows are made.

About Horsehair

When viewed with the naked eye, horsehair appears to be smooth, but under examination with a microscope, the surface of the hair is quite rough. Particles called follicles project from the hair and form an abrasive surface. Rosin, a tree sap derivative, is applied to bow hair to increase its gripping power. When rosined bow hair is drawn across a string on an instrument, the hair grips the string and excites it into motion causing the vibration that produces a tone.

As the bow is drawn across a string, the bow hair appears to be in constant contact with the string. However, this is not the case. Instead, what is occurring is that the bow hair is gripping and releasing the string in a rapid sequence replicating a plucking action. This action causes the string to be drawn to a point where its lateral tension is sufficient to over-come the gripping force of the rosined bow hair (Fig. 2.5 B).

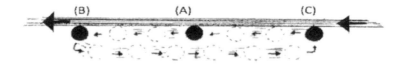

Figure 2.5   Bow Hair String Contact

When the string reaches that point, it releases itself from the bow and returns to cross its point of equilibrium (Fig. 2.5 A), proceeds to its oppo-site lateral extreme (Fig. 2.5 C), only to be gripped again by the bow hair and then to repeat the process. The final effect is one of a string gripped by the bow hair, pulled to a point of tension, breaking free from that grip, rebounding to a point opposite that from which it was just released, and then being caught again by the bow hair, only to start the process again. All of this occurs in such rapid succession that it is invisible to the naked eye.

Tuning – The Process
To learn the tuning process for these instruments, see chapter 7.

The Open Strings
The strings on violin, viola, and cello are tuned in fifths. The double bass is tuned in fourths. Starting from the lowest string, the instruments are tuned as follows:

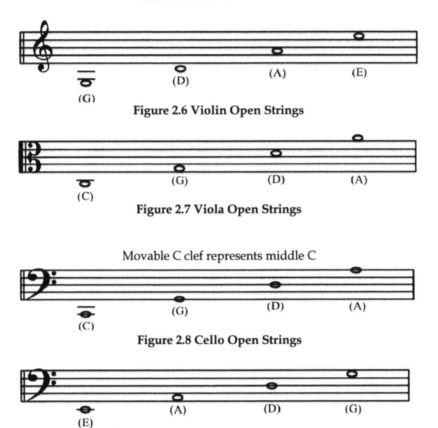

Figure 2.6 Violin Open Strings

Figure 2.7 Viola Open Strings

Movable C clef represents middle C

Figure 2.8 Cello Open Strings

Figure 2.9 Double Bass Open Strings
The double bass sounds one octave below the written notes.

Fingering

The fingering patterns for the violin, viola, and cello are almost identical. The player is able to raise the pitch of each string in half steps or in any interval up to seven steps above the open string by depressing the string to the fingerboard with the fingers of the left hand (Fig. 2.10).

Figure 2.10 Fingering

Positions

The term *positions* refers to the placement of a player's fingers on an instrument's fingerboard in relation to the open string.
The following chart is a guide to these labels for the violin and viola (Fig. 2.11):

First Finger Placement	Position Name
Half step	Half
Whole step	First
One and a half steps	Second
Two and a half steps	Third
Three and a half steps	Fourth
Four steps	Fifth
Five steps	Sixth
Six steps	Seventh

Figure 2.11 Intervals

The patterns for the violin and viola are the same except for the distance between the fingers. The distance between each finger can be adjusted to produce either a half step or whole step. Adding fingers adds steps. Adding multiple fingers produces intervals. Fingering for the cello follows the same pattern except that there is a half position for every full

pattern is as follows: ½, 1st, 2nd, 2 ½, 3rd, 3 ½, 4th, 5th, 5 ½, 6th, 6 ½, and 7th. Each of these positions progresses by half steps up to the seventh position. Note that whereas violinist and violist can play five half steps in each position, the cellist can play only three half steps. There are no half positions for the first and fourth positions because of the natural half step between E and F and B and C in the diatonic scale.

Fingering for the double bass follows a slightly different pattern since its larger size requires a greater spread between notes and because the ring finger is not used alone but in conjunction with the pinky. Used individually, the ring finger and pinky both lack strength.

The pattern for the positions on the double bass, starting from an open string is: ½, 1st, 2nd, 2½, 3rd, 3½, 4th, 5th, 5½, 6th, 6½, and 7th. Each of these positions progresses by half steps up to the seventh position. Note that the double bass player is restricted to playing only three half steps in a position because the third and fourth fingers are used in combination. Similar to the cello, there are no half positions for the first and fourth positions because of the natural half step between E and F, and B and C in the diatonic scale.

The following pages contain basic fingering charts for the violin, viola, cello, and double bass. More extensive fingering charts are available on the internet and in printed publications. Google Fingering Charts for String Instruments.

To finger a note, press the string at the position noted on the chart using the fingers indicated at the left.

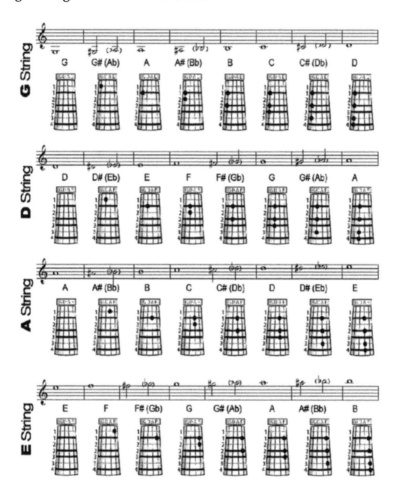

Figure 2.12 Basic Violin Fingering Chart

To finger a note, press the string at the position noted on the chart and use the fingers indicated at the left. The notes in this chart are written in the alto clef where the third line represents middle C.

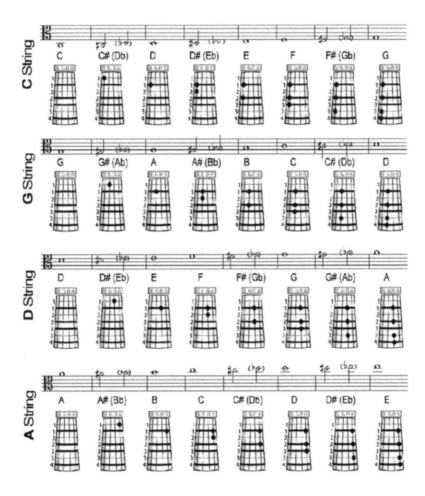

Figure 2.13 Basic Viola Fingering Chart

To finger a note, press the string at the position noted on the charts and use the fingers indicated at the left.

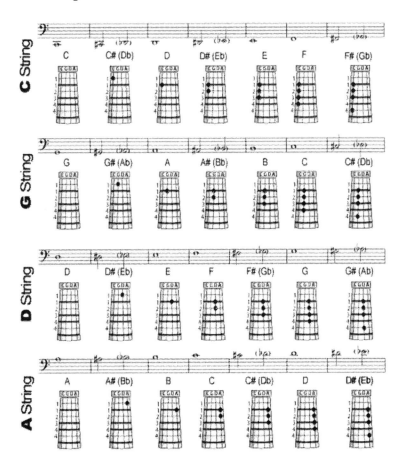

Figure 2.14 Basic Cello Fingering Chart

To finger a note, press the string at the position noted on the chart and use the finger indicated at the left.

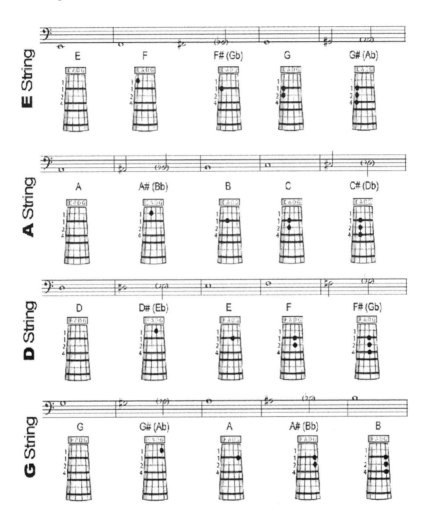

Figure 2.15 Basic Double Bass Fingering Chart

Producing Sound

There are several ways to produce sounds on violin family instruments. Most common is by drawing a wooden bow strung with horsehair across a string. The player can also pluck the strings with the right or left hand, or bounce the stick side of the bow on the string or draw it across the strings to produce a special effect. The term used for playing with the wooden stick is called *con legno,* Italian for with the wood.

Holding the Bow

The following is one recommended way to hold a bow when playing the violin, viola, and cello. The final position arrived at for holding a bow or for playing any instrument is the result of the individuality of the player's physical makeup and the position which is most effective and comfortable for the player. Notice the violations of all rules at the next live performance you attend.

1. With your left hand, pick up the bow by the center of the stick with the frog facing your right hand.

2. Bend your right thumb in at the first knuckle and position your thumb between the hair and the stick with your thumb gently pressing into the bow grip (Fig. 2.16).

Figure 2.16 Bow Holding Position

3. Rest your index finger at the first knuckle on the opposite side of the stick and slightly forward of your thumb.

4. Allow your pinky to fall naturally, with a slight arch, on the screw end of the bow. The exact point where you are able to balance the bow will be the correct placement for each individual. Your thumb, index finger, and pinky are the three fingers that control the balance of the bow (Fig. 2.17).

Figure 2.17   Bow Holding Position

5. Allow your middle and fourth fingers to fall naturally on the outer side of the stick.

6. While holding the stick in this manner, adjust your finger positions to that which will allow you to have best control over the bow.

The two types of bow used to play the double bass are the French and German bows. The French style double bass bow is held in the same manner as that of the violin, viola, and cello. The German style bass bow (Fig. 2.18) has a frog that requires a grip different from that of the other bows.

Figure 2.18 German Bass Bow

For the German bass bow:

1. Hold the bow by the stick with your left hand and place the frog in the palm of your right hand with the screw extending between your thumb and index finger.

2. Place your thumb around the top of the bow stick and your pinky finger on the underside of the frog.

3. Allow your middle and ring fingers to comfortably grip the inside of the frog.

4. Strive to adjust your grip in such a manner as to have complete control of the bow with a firm yet relaxed hold. Each grip will be individual (Fig. 2.19).

Figure 2.19   German Bass Bow Holding Position

Strings

Chapter 8 on accessories tells of the different types of strings that are available and the various attributes of each. Among the most common products used to make strings are gut, steel, perlon (a type of plastic fiber), silk, chromium/steel, and gold. Each type of string construction produces a different sound quality and can alter the overall tone quality of an instrument. The choice of strings, therefore, becomes a matter worthy of great consideration. Chapter 8 will help you make that decision.

Structural Differences
The Violin

Structural differences among these instruments, aside from their size and playing range, are slight and the instruments work in much the same way. The violin is the most acoustically perfect of the four. The viola, cello, and double bass are progressively (but not proportionately) larger while still maintaining essentially the same structure and design of the violin. However, their acoustical perfection does wane as their sizes increase.

The Viola

The viola is often described as being a large violin because both instruments share many characteristics of design, physics, construction, and appearance. The instrument is tuned a fifth lower than the violin but is one-seventh larger, making the difference in pitch disproportionate to the difference in size. This ratio of tuning to size results in the darker timbre associated with the viola. While the body of a full size violin is almost always the same size, 14 inches (35.5 cm) long, the size of a viola body can vary as much as four inches. Viola body sizes can range from 13½ inches to 17½ inches in length with widths ranging proportionate to the length.

Another difference between the violin and viola appears in the size-to-pitch ratio. An instrument which is tuned a perfect fifth below the violin should be considerably larger than the viola if it were to follow the size-to-pitch ratio set by the design of the violin. In fact, the size of the viola should be so great that it would not be manageable as an instrument to be played under the chin. Since the viola is not correctly proportioned to its tuning, viola makers can enjoy a bit of latitude when designing the instrument and can alter the size to produce the tone quality desired.

The Cello

The cello, or violoncello, is also disproportionate in size to its difference in tuning. It is tuned a full octave below the viola but the cello is smaller than its acoustical requirement. The discrepancy is compensated for by a significant increase in the depth or thickness of the body of the instrument. With the increased depth, the lower tones are able to resonate with the characteristic cello timbre. Because of its relatively large size, the cello is supported by an end pin that extends from the bottom of the instrument (Fig. 2.20). The end pin is adjustable to accommodate different size players.

Figure 2.20   Cello End Pin

The cello rests with its end pin on the floor while the player balances the instrument between the knees. In this position, the strings are reversed from those on the violin and viola. In playing position the lowest string, the C string, now becomes the first string on the right hand of the player as opposed to violins and violas in playing position which have the highest string at the player's right side.

The Double Bass

The double bass is the lowest-sounding instrument of the violin family. Although it also shares the principles of the string instrument design, the double bass has the greatest structural differences of the family.

As stated above, double bass pegs are neither made of wood nor do they function on the wooden wedge principle. Because of the greater thickness of the strings, there is need for a stronger and more stable peg. This necessity produced the worm and gear system now used exclusively on this instrument (Fig. 2.21).

Figure 2.21 Double Bass and Gear System

This system is used on fretted string instruments and can be installed on any of the other three instruments of the violin family. Such a modification is usually restricted to use on student instruments, since the worm and gear mechanism helps facilitate the tuning of a string instrument. Unfortunately, the mechanism adds a considerable amount of weight to the peg box and consequently the advantages of easier tuning are outweighed by a possible problem of balance on the violin or viola. The use of the worm and gear system is more practical on the cello and the double bass since these instruments rest on the floor and balance is less of a burden to the player.

In addition to its larger size, the double bass differs slightly in shape from the three smaller instruments. While the shoulders of these instruments are at a 90 degree angle from the fingerboard, the size of the double bass requires that the shoulders be sloped in order to allow the player to reach the higher playing positions comfortably (Fig. 2.22).

Figure 2.22 Double Bass Shoulders

Another difference is found in the back of some double basses. Rather than being rounded, the back of the larger instrument starts out from the heel of the neck sloping outward and then levels off to a flat back for the major portion of the instrument (Fig. 2.23). This design allows the maker to use less than half of the wood required for a rounded back without sacrificing any structural integrity.

Figure 2.23   Double Bass Back

Some double basses have a fifth string enabling the performer to play down to C, a third below the lowest string on the instrument. An additional way to achieve this extended range is to install a device that lowers the pitch of the fourth string to C. Read more about this in chapter 8.

Construction

All the instruments in the violin family are constructed using similar designs, acoustical principles, and manufacturing techniques. The violin, the most acoustically perfect of the four, will be used as a model for a study of the entire family. The viola, cello, and double bass are progressively (but not proportionately) larger while still maintaining essentially the same structure and design as the violin. These instruments are a model of simplicity composed of shaped wooden wedges, plates, and strips which support the strings and permit the player to shorten the open strings in order to raise the pitches from the original tuning.

Figure 2.24 is a diagram of a violin naming the exterior parts. The mechanism that supports the strings starting from the top of the instrument consists of the scroll (A), peg box (B), pegs (C), neck (D), fingerboard (E), bridge (F), saddle (G), tailpiece (H), tailgut (I), and end button (J).

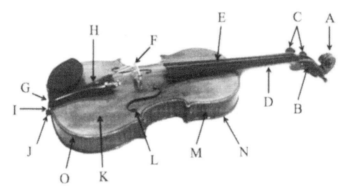

Figure 2.24 Violin Parts

The body of the instrument is made up of a top (K), "f" holes (L), sides (M), a back (N), and purfling (O) surrounding the top and back plates. These parts form the exterior of the body.

Inside the instrument (Fig. 2.25), supporting the exterior, are the ribs and linings (A), top and bottom block (B), corner blocks (C), bass bar (D), and sound post (E).

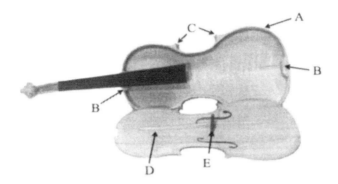

Figure 2.25 Violin Interior

The violin and viola share all of the parts described above. The cello differs in that it does not have a chin rest for obvious reasons and has an end pin in place of the violin's end button. The end pin is shown in Figure 2.20.

The double bass also differs from the violin in that, like the cello, it too has an adjustable end pin. Another significant difference is found in the worm and gear machine head tuning device which is almost exclusive to the double bass because of the thickness of the strings. See Figure 2.24 for more details on this topic.

Materials

The materials most commonly used for the construction of these instruments are spruce, maple, ebony, and rosewood. The tops are generally made of spruce, a softer wood which fills the design requirements for the most effective sound amplification. Spruce is also used for the sound post, linings, and the bass bar.

The back, sides, neck, and scroll are generally made of hard maple, again in compliance with the prescription for achieving the most responsive amplifier while maintaining structural integrity. Hard maple or a wood of similar strength is needed to support the tension exerted by the strings stretched across the instrument.

The trim on the instrument (Fig. 2.26), namely, the end button (A), saddle (B), tailpiece (C), fingerboard (D), nut (E), and pegs (F), is usually made of ebony, rosewood, or, in the case of low-quality instruments, less expensive hardwoods, metal, or plastic.

Figure 2.26 Instrument Trim

All of these instruments are constructed of the same materials and essentially use the same technology in practically the same way. The only difference is in the size and proportions of the larger instruments. For less expensive larger instruments, laminated wood is used to cut costs while improving the instrument's structural integrity.

There are two ways in which wood can be cut for use to make the upper and lower plates (top and back respectively) of the violin. If it is the intention of the maker to construct an instrument with a two piece back plate, the wood is cut into a triangular shaped block which is then cut vertically down the middle to form two triangles (Fig. 2.27). These are then joined to form one plate that is subsequently carved into shape. This process is used in order to increase the likelihood of achieving a symmetrical wood grain pattern.

Figure 2.27 Wedge Shaped Wood Cut

The second possibility is to cut a layer of wood that will produce a one piece plate. This method eliminates the seam from the middle of the plate (Fig. 2.28). The disadvantage of this method is the likelihood that a one piece slab of wood, because of the span of the size required, will have a variation in grain as the cut progresses. It is more desirable to maintain a uniform grain in these plates for esthetic and acoustic reasons. The triangle cut maintains this uniformity because the cuts are taken from a smaller portion of the overall slab of wood.

Figure 2.28 Cross Cut Wood Cut

Strings – A number of different materials are currently used to manufacture strings. Chapter 8 on accessories covers this topic in more detail.

The Bridge

When a bow is properly drawn across a string, the sound that is generated is conducted to the top or belly of the instrument by the bridge (Fig. 2.29). As the string vibrates, its transverse (side to side) motion is converted by the bridge into a perpendicular (up and down) "stamping" motion. The feet of the bridge transfer the vibrations to the belly of the instrument.

Figure 2.29 Bridge

Since the bridge plays a dominant role in transferring the sound from the string to the amplifier (body) of the instrument, the design and material used to make the bridge and its placement on the instrument must be calculated to fill that function in the best way. Chapter 7 explains the details of bridge placement and dimensions.

The Sound Post and Bass Bar

The sound post (Fig. 2.30) plays an important role in sound transmission. In addition to acting as a structural support for the top of the instrument, this post, made of soft wood, conducts the vibrations from the top of the instrument to its back. The sound post distributes tones produced by the higher strings to the back of the instrument while muting any echo effect which would occur if that post were not present.

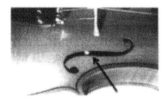

Figure 2.30 Sound Post

The bass bar (Fig. 2.31) serves two functions. Located on the under-side of the top of the instrument directly beneath the bridge foot for lower strings, the bass bar reinforces the instrument, supporting the great force exerted by the tension of the strings. It also distributes the vibrations lat-erally throughout the top.

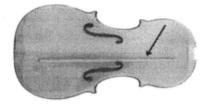

Figure 2.31 Bass Bar

The sound post and bass bar together distribute sound throughout the body. This distribution acts as an amplifier for the sounds generated by the strings. The motion of the components stimulates the air pocket con-tained within the body into vibrating patterns of compression and rare-faction. See chapter 12 on The Science of Sound. The sound generated at the string is transported through the bridge, belly, sound post, and bass bar to ultimately produce the tone of the instrument.

The Sides and Back

The sides and back of the instrument are usually made of maple. This is a harder wood than spruce which is used for the belly of the violin. The function of the sides and back, in addition to enhancing the vibrating process, is to form the supporting structure for the entire instrument. The tension incurred by the strings stretched from the top (pegs) to the bot-tom (tailpiece), some 68 lbs. (31 kg) for the violin, draws the top (scroll end) and bottom of the instrument (tailpiece end) toward each other. It is the strength of the back plate combined with the sides that prevent the instrument from folding in half.

On the double bass there is some variation to the design of the back plate. In addition to following the traditional design as found in the other three violin family instruments, some double basses are constructed with a flat back pictured and described in Figure 2.26 above.

"F" Holes and Purfling

There are two parts of the sound amplifier that appear to be ornamental but in fact play an important role in the production of sound. These are the sound holes or "f" holes so named because of their shape and the purfling which appears to be an ornamental trim inlaid around the edge of the top and back of the body.

The "f" holes (Fig. 2.32) significantly affect the quality of the tone of the instrument. The flexing action of the mid portion of the top and the ability of the tone-saturated air within the sound box to escape are affected by the size, shape, and location of the holes. Because of the importance of these shapely orifices, their exact shape, size, and location are distinct to each craftsman.

Figure 2.32 F Holes

Purfling (Fig. 2.33) is made of two parallel strips of hard wood, usually ebony, which are inlaid into the surface around the edge of the top and back of the violin. Purfling serves an important acoustical purpose. The groove cut for the inlay acts as a barrier or interruption for the vibration that is traveling through the wood. Through the use of purfling, the maker is able to define clearly the area throughout which the vibration is to take place and thereby control that vibrating area and the tone it produces.

Figure 2.33 Purfling

A Review of How They Work

The complete amplifying process on the instruments of the violin family is shown in Figure 2.34 below. The string's vibrations (1) are conducted by the hardwood (usually maple) bridge (2) to the softer wood (usually spruce) top plate (3). The vibrations are then transported via the softwood sound post (4) to the hardwood back (5) of the instrument and via the softwood bass bar (6) laterally throughout the entire top.

Figure 2.34 Instrument Parts

The hardwood back and softer wood top (belly) are joined by hardwood sides (7). Combined, the top, sides, and back form an air space in which the sound circulates. The interaction of all of these components forms the amplifier for the sound produced by the strings. The combined motion of these parts sets the volume of air contained within the body of the instrument into a pumping motion that forces the resonating sound out of the instrument through the "f" holes. In this manner the instruments produce sound.

Summary

In spite of the more than three-hundred-year history of the violin, the exact interaction which takes place among these components is not yet fully understood. The mathematical simplicity and consistency of the design of the instrument become evident when one observes that violins hardly vary in their proportions.

The greatest amount of wood is found beneath the bridge. The thickness of the wood decreases to half the amount at the sides of the instrument while remaining consistent throughout the length of the bass bar. Farther across the top of the instrument, the measurement at the thinnest part of the top becomes equal to one quarter of the thickest part. The ratios then progress from the whole (thickest) to one-half of the whole (medium), and then to one quarter of the whole (thinnest).

The amplifier or body of these instruments is deceptive in its simple appearance and yet they utilize a most complex system for distributing vibrations. The vibrations are carried throughout the physical structure of the wooden body and travel in every direction. This diversity of movement causes the instrument to vibrate and oscillate horizontally, vertically, and diagonally. Simultaneously, the air contained within the body is set into motion, increasing and decreasing in volume while traveling in and out of the body through the "f" holes.

The main function of the bodies of woodwind and brass instruments is to contain the columns of air that are set into motion and act as a structure into which various mechanical devices are incorporated to extend or shorten that vibrating air column. In the case of the violin family, the body acts as the amplifier of sound that profoundly affects the quality of tone produced and has no part in the changing of pitch. Of course that is achieved by the player's fingers shortening (stopping) the strings.

An expertly crafted violin strung with an appropriate set of strings and played with a good quality bow will produce a better tone than a poorer quality instrument set up with the same bow and strings. Unlike wind instruments, the tone quality of string instruments is largely a product of the quality of the material used in the construction of the body of the instrument and of the design and craftsmanship used in making the instrument.

The violin, viola, cello, and double bass, sharing most of the same technology, combine to make the most versatile choir of instruments in the contemporary music world. These instruments are similar in design, acoustical function, construction, and history. They enjoy a romantic quality that has resulted in their being considered collectibles, works of art, a three-century-old mystery story, and the heart of the modern symphony orchestra.

Chapter 3
Different Kinds of Violins, Violas,
Cellos, and Double Basses

This chapter will introduce the reader to related members of the violin family and the different iterations of those instruments which will thereby provide a broader perspective to possibly expanding playing experiences in the future.

Four Kinds of Instruments of the Violin Family

As of this writing, the four most popular kinds of violins, violas, cellos, and double basses on the market are contemporary or modern, Baroque past and present, modified, and electric.

Contemporary Instruments

The contemporary violin family instruments consist of those we all know and use in present-day study and performance. They are a derivative of instruments developed during the Baroque period, the original patterns used in the sixteenth through eighteenth centuries. For a description of how the contemporary instruments differ from the Baroque designs, see chapter 1. To learn how the contemporary instruments function, see chapter 2.

Baroque Instruments

Baroque instruments are named for the period in which they were built. Between the sixteenth and eighteenth centuries, instrument making was evolutionary, experimental, and transitional. Experimentation rather than standardization was the rule of the day. The violins and violas of that period had a shorter thicker neck, which was the primary means of supporting the instrument. The chin rest and shoulder rest had not yet been invented. The fingerboard was also shorter than that of the contemporary violin and viola and ran almost parallel to the top of the instrument. The contemporary violin neck slants down in relation to the violin top resulting in a gradual upward projection of the fingerboard. Figure 3.1 shows a Baroque model with the flatter configuration followed by a contemporary pattern with the neck slanting down.

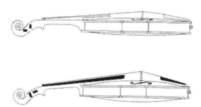

Figure 3.1 Baroque and Modern Violin Configurations

The cellos and double basses of that period were less consistent in their design than the violins and violas were because these larger instruments were less in demand, fewer were made, and they were more in the developmental stage than were their smaller cousins. The cello was a derivative of the viola da gamba, a big viola which, when played, was held between the knees. The double bass makers were also going through a period of experimentation where, in many cases, individual instruments were made to provide for a particular musical circumstance. Standardization had not yet begun.

The Baroque bridge (Fig. 3.2), as compared to the modern bridge, was lower, had a much more open design, and had eyes (holes carved in the bridge) that were higher or closer to a thicker top. The larger eyes compensated for the greater mass, permitting the bridge to vibrate more readily. Because of that design, the sound was directed from the vibrating strings down to the top of the instrument producing an increase in the upper partials in relation to the fundamental pitch while adding resonance and warmth to the tone. The resulting tone quality was fuller in harmonic content but lacking in brilliance. The more mellow sound was the preferred violin tone of that time. Because there were no standard patterns for any of these instruments experimentation with a great deal of trial and error was the theme of the era.

Figure 3.2 Baroque and Modern Bridges

The Bass Bar

The bass bar is described in chapter 2 as a strip of wood, most often spruce, which is installed on the underside of the top of an instrument directly under the bridge foot of the lowest string (Fig. 3.3). The two functions of the bass bar are to help distribute the lower pitches produced by those strings throughout the instrument and to support the pressure exerted by the tuned strings on the instrument's top.

Figure 3.3 Bass Bar

When all four strings of an instrument are tuned, they exert a great deal of pressure on the top. During the Baroque period, most strings were made of animal entrails (gut), a soft, pliable product. The early instruments were originally built with a bass bar of sufficient strength to support that tension. As man-made products such as steel, rope core, and perlon began to be used to make strings, the pressure on the top of the instruments increased to the point where there was a need to support the added pressure. This situation led to some experimentation to expand the bass bar and increase its ability to support the additional load. The bass bar on instruments of the past had to be replaced with one that was considerably longer and with a deeper center section. Presently, there are almost no Baroque instruments that have retained their original bass bars.

The Sound Post

The sound post is a dowel-shaped piece of wood that is placed inside the body of a string instrument under the left foot of the bridge. It is wedged in between the top and back of the instrument and held in place by the pressure exerted on the instrument's top by the tension of the tuned strings. Sound posts are not glued in place.

Like the bass bar, the function of the sound post is two-fold. It supports the pressure exerted on the instrument's top by the tuned strings and distributes the vibrations of the higher pitched notes throughout the instrument's body (Fig. 3.4). In the original Baroque instruments, the sound post was of a small diameter. As the higher tension strings evolved, it was decided to increase the diameter of the sound post to support that increased pressure while conducting the sounds of the higher strings. The Italian name for the sound post is "anima" or the "soul" reflecting its extraordinary influence on the sound of an instrument.

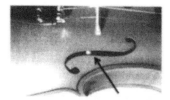

Figure 3.4 Sound Post

Most Baroque instruments used gut strings which were attached to a tailpiece that was much flatter than that of the contemporary design and had round holes rather than the keyhole shape holes now in use (Fig. 3.5). There was no upper saddle on the tailpiece. As a result the strings lay flat and parallel to the fingerboard. Fine tuners did not exist and were not needed because there were no high-tension steel or Perlon strings in existence at that time.

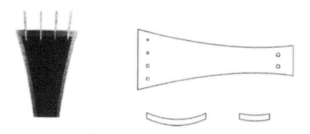

Figure 3.5 Baroque Tailpiece

Modified Instruments

A modified instrument is one that has been altered in size or design to accommodate for the special needs or desires of the player.

Different Size Violins

The introduction of the Suzuki string teaching method in the mid-twentieth century led to a demand for different size instruments of the violin family. The Suzuki method begins students at the earliest possible age, in some cases even before they are able to speak. To accommodate these young people, violins were produced in nine different sizes graduated down to as small as 1/32 size. The violin sizes now available are named in fractions as follows. 4/4 = 23", 3/4 = 22", 1/2 = 20", 1/4 = 18", 1/8th = 16", 1/10 = 15", 1/16 = 14" and 1/32 = 13." One additional size, the ninth one that has been available for centuries, is the 7/8th or "lady size" violin, which has a 13 ½" body.

The fractional names do not represent the actual relationships to the 4/4 full size instrument but are just names given to identify the various gradations. The fractional named sizes can vary from maker to maker in actual inches to as much as half an inch in either direction. It is therefore recommended when acquiring an instrument that the player physically tries it and, if possible, under the supervision of the teacher. A Viometer measuring device can be used by the teacher or instrument dealer to ensure an accurate measurement. If that is not possible, be sure there is a return or exchange option in the arrangement made with the dealer.

Different Size Violas

Violas, cellos, and double basses have also been re-sized to accommodate younger students. However, the manufacturers of these instruments have not standardized the size changes and dimensions to the degree of those of the violin makers. As a result, a bit more judgment is needed in determining a correct size for a young student of one of these three instruments.

In the case of the viola, the instruments are sized in inches as opposed to the "non-fractional" fractions used for the violin. Measuring the body alone, violas graduate from a body of 12" (equal to a ½ size violin), 13" (equal to a ¾ size violin), 14" (equal to a full size violin), and then 15", 15 ½", 16", and 16 ½." There are some violas that are still larger, graduating in half-inch increments up to 18." These are usually used by professional performers. Again, one must be aware of the possibility of some slight variations in these dimensions, depending on the maker.

Often, when 12, 13, and 14 inch violas are not available, a dealer, with the approval of the teacher, will re-string a half, three quarter, or full size violin with a viola setup to fill the need. This adjustment is a satisfactory arrangement except for the fact that the depth of those violins is a bit shallower than would be a viola of the same size. The result of this condition is a small loss of the depth of tone associated with the viola sound. In most cases in the early stages of instruction, this loss would be of little consequence and would be made up as the instrument sizes increased to true viola sizes.

Different Size Cellos

Cellos also use the fraction format to identify the different sizes. In keeping with the consistency of inconsistency paradigm found throughout the musical instrument industry, one will find cellos with the same size label having different dimensions. In these cases the difference in body length between what is referred to as the European size compared to that of the Suzuki measurements will be on average from one to three inches.

The measurements in inches for cello body length are as follows:

Size	European	Suzuki
Full size	30 inches	30 inches
Three Quarter	27 ¼ inches	26 inches
One half	26 inches	23 inches
One quarter	23 inches	20 inches
One eighth	20 inches	17¾ inches (equal to the one tenth European size)
One tenth	17 ¾	N/A

Because of these sometimes significant size differences, it is recommended that when acquiring an instrument, the player physically tries it and, if possible, under the supervision of the teacher. If that is not possible, be sure there is a return or exchange option in the arrangement made with the dealer.

Different Size Double Basses

The double bass enjoys even more latitude in the manner in which the different sizes are labeled. One would think a full 4/4 size double bass is the size of choice for an adult, but that is not the case. The most commonly used bass is the three quarter 3/4 size for reasons unknown to anyone. Unlike the violin, viola, and cello, it appears that the makers of double basses enjoy a freedom in pattern design and dimension that is not available to the luthiers of the smaller instruments of the violin family. For an illustration of this disparity in sizing see www.gollihurmusic.com on line.

Figure 3.6 illustrates the relaxed attitude of individual double bass makers with regard to standardizing their dimensions. On the other hand, one might conclude with some degree of assurance that the mass producers of double basses tend to adhere to some size consistency in order to satisfy the general double bass player student population.

Luthiers who make instruments for specific bassists or just as a handmade instrument for sale will sometimes deviate from what may be considered standard sizing in order to achieve a specific acoustical effect.

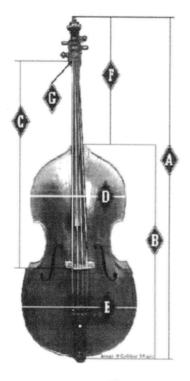

	4/4	¾	¾ Kay	½	1/4
A	74.8	71.6	71.6	65.7	61.4
B	45.7	43.7	43.7	40.2	37.4
C	43.3	41.3	41.5	38	35.4
D	21.3	20.3	20.25	18.7	17.3
E	26.8	25.6	26.5	23.6	21.9
F	30.9	29.5	28.	27.2	25.2
G	1.8	1.7	1.6	1.6	1.5

Figure 3.6 Double Bass Dimension Chart
(Reproduced with permission of the Gollihur Music Co.)

The E String Extension

Relatively few orchestrations call for the double bass to play notes below the open low E string, the lowest string on a traditional bass, but
there is an occasional need for those notes. To accommodate for that situation, some instruments are made with a fifth string which is tuned to C
or B below the low E string. If an instrument lacks this fifth string and the
player must use the lower range, an extension can be added to the instrument. This device makes it possible to use a longer string in place of
the low E string so the player can reach low B.

There are a number ways to achieve this end. If one is considering this
addition, it is strongly advised that due diligence be applied to a search
for the luthier who will best satisfy the needs of the player. Luthiers who
specialize in designing and installing extensions usually have their own
variations of the installation process. Figure 3.7 illustrates two different
extensions.

Figure 3.7 Double Bass Extensions

Left Handed Instruments

Another modification of the original structure of violin family instruments is used to adapt instruments for left-handed players. There has
been an ongoing dispute among musicians and educators regarding the
need to modify an instrument for left-handed players. One point of view
is that the natural playing position of the traditional non fretted string
instrument centers on the left hand as being predominant since it is used
to finger all the notes. As is the case with all musical instruments, both
hands are used to play them. There are no left-handed clarinets, trumpets,
etc., so why do we need left-handed string instruments?

In contrast to this line of thinking is the belief that the musician's use of the bow is the predominant facilitator of the bowed instrument sound. The player controls the sound production in terms of volume, tone production, stylistic nuance, and overall virtuosity through the action of the bow. If this is indeed the case, the player would be at an advantage using his or her predominant hand and arm for the bow.

A left-handed bowed instrument must in every sense be a mirror image of a traditional instrument. The left handed instrument has the strings located in reverse order so that the highest string on a violin and viola is located on the left side of the instrument and the opposite is the case for the cello and double bass. The other strings then follow suit from left to right. The lowest string for the violin and viola is on the player's right side and for the cello and double bass on the left side. With the strings reversed, it becomes necessary to reverse the pegs in the peg box. The pegs that are on the right side must be switched to the left and vice versa.

It then follows that all the other sound controlling and amplifying parts of the instrument must also be reversed. The sound post and bass bar locations must be switched to allow them to fulfill their sound-conducting duties. The bass bar, normally on the left side under the lower strings, is moved to the right for the new location of those strings. The sound post is moved to the left side to pick up the higher frequency strings and distribute those sounds throughout the instrument.

A well-made bridge is shaped differently from one side to the other, with the lower side being on the highest string. The string grooves on the bridge are cut to accommodate the different thickness of the strings. A bridge cut for a left-handed violin must be cut with the same specifications but as a mirror image of the traditional "right handed" bridge.

Continuing down to the lower part of the instrument for the violin and viola, a left-handed chin rest must be used and some adjustments made to the tailpiece. Any fine tuners that may be included on that part of the instrument must be relocated to accommodate the changed location of the strings. The cello and double bass will not need any adjustment to the end pins. However, if an extension for the addition of a fifth string on the double bass is part of an instrument, it, too, must be relocated to the opposite side.

Amplified (Electric) Instruments

Electric or amplified instruments of the violin family are, by comparison, still in the early stages of development. Although these instruments first appeared in the 1920s, their development languished over a seventy-year period until the 1990s when interest in them began to take hold. Having not yet found their way into the classical music repertoire, they are primarily used in venues that feature popular orchestral music in the lyrical style.

An electric violin, viola, cello, or double bass is capable of all the electronic special effects associated with the electric guitar because they share the same basic sound modification equipment. These include pick-ups of assorted types, pre-amplifiers, amplifiers, equalizers, and speakers.

Acoustic Electric Instruments

The two types of electric instruments are the acoustic and the solid body. An acoustic electric instrument is a traditional instrument to which a pickup is added. Some types of pickups are the piezoelectric bridges (a form of electronic frequency generator), body pickups, a magnetic pickup attached to the bridge, body, or the end or underside of the fingerboards, or a microphone. These can be attached to the bridge, the body, or the end, or underside of the fingerboard. The pickups are connected with a cable to an amplifier using the same equipment as is used for the electric guitar.

Acoustic instruments are built with a sound amplifying body and can use any of the pickups described above to produce an adequate result; however, because the body is a resonating cavity, there is a greater chance of feedback. There is also the problem of the pickup amplifying all the sounds that are associated with handling the instrument such as bumps, knocks, and in some cases even the actual fingering of the notes on the fingerboard.

A bridge pickup using a piezoelectric contact can be mounted in various ways. A piezo pickup can be placed under one or both feet of the bridge (Fig. 3.8). The disadvantage of this pickup is that it interferes with the bridge's direct contact with the instrument's top, slightly lessening the non-amplified sound production of the instrument. This type of pickup is best used for continuous amplified playing only.

Figure 3.8 Piezo Pickup

There are bridges that are constructed with a piezo element for each string built into the bridge (Fig. 3.9). When each string is in direct contact with its own amplifying element a better sound will result.

Figure 3.9 Built-in Element

A modification of the "one element for each string type" bridge offers adjustable feet for the bridge to ensure a better fit on the top of the instrument (Fig. 3.10).

Figure 3.10 Adjustable Feet Bridge

A piezo element inserted in a very thin slice of wood can be installed on the wing slots of the bridge (Fig. 3.11).

Figure 3.11 Wing Pickup

A piezo wafer contact can be placed under each bridge foot and an additional contact can be connected to the center cutout of the bridge (Fig. 3.12).

Figure 3.12 Three Point Pickup

A single contact can be placed in the center of the bridge and connected to a volume control clamped onto the violin body (Fig. 3.13).

Figure 3.13 Single Pickup

The bimorphic pickup is a solid bridge modified with a cutout between each string slot so the strings are independent and separated from each other (Fig. 3.14). This design allows each string to vibrate freely with little or no interference or restriction from surrounding bridge material or adjacent strings. A sensor called a Bimorphic Piezoelectric Bender Sensor is inserted into each freestanding segment so the string, supported by its own freestanding piezo-containing segment of bridge, has greater vibration flexibility.

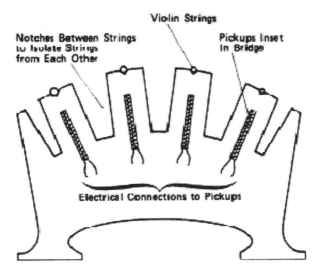

Figure 3.14 Bimorphic Pickup

The Band is the name given to a pickup that is wrapped around the body of an instrument below the bridge and is held in place by Velcro (Fig. 3.15).

Figure 3.15 Band Pickup

An Omni directional miniature microphone that clips on to the strings between the tailpiece and bridge can be fitted on instruments using mounting hardware specifically designed for that purpose. This microphone is considered by some to produce an exceptionally good sound (Fig. 3.16).

Figure 3.16 Omni Directional Pickup

Solid Body Electric Instrument

Solid body electric instruments in the violin family share the same attributes as those of the solid body guitar. The pickups are built into the instrument along with a cable jack, volume control, and in some cases, an equalizer. This design both solves and creates a problem.

Acoustic instruments that are converted to electric amplification often produce a feedback caused by the resonance of the hollow body. The solid body eliminates that problem by electronically transporting the sound directly from the instrument's strings to the amplifier. However, the addition of the wood or other material used to make the instrument's body solid increases its weight to the point where it can be a distraction to the player. Solid body instruments are more durable and less expensive than the adapted acoustic instrument.

In an effort to deal with the problem of the extra weight a solid body can add to an instrument, a number of modifications have been made. The results have been some rather unique products that resemble a violin, viola, cello, or double bass but in many cases only in the most remote fashion. They all have at least four strings (although some have five or more): a tuning mechanism, fingerboard, bridge, tailpiece, and a chin rest where needed. Substitutes for wood in making the solid body include carbon fiber, Kevlar and other forms of glass and carbon-based materials.

Electric Violins

Figure 3.17 shows only a few of the many different design solid body violins that are available. The uniqueness of shapes is limited only by one's imagination.

Figure 3.17 Solid Body Electric Violins

Electric Violas

Electric violas, both acoustic and solid body, share the same construction, design flexibility, and amplification devices as those of the electric violin. Figure 3.18 shows examples of electric solid body violas. The difference between the electric violin and viola would be found in any amplifying accommodation an individual would make to enhance the lower sounds in the viola register.

Figure 3.18 Solid Body Violas

Electric Cellos

Solid body electric cellos began to appear in the mid to late 1990s. Their popularity can be attributed to their comparatively low cost, ease of maintenance, sturdy, lightweight construction, smaller size, and portability. These instruments use the same amplification systems as do the solid body violins and violas with one exception. In an effort to make the sound a solid body electric cello produces closer to that of an acoustic model, some solid body instruments have a small hollowed-out area which contains oscillators to enhance the tone quality. This process is successful to some degree; however, electronic systems are not able to produce the complex upper partials or harmonics of a pitch produced by an acoustic cello. While the timbre of the electric solid body cello does resemble that of its acoustic cousin, a listener with a "good ear" will be less than satisfied.

The elimination of the need for a resounding chamber, i.e., the body of the cello, and the intent to make these instruments as durable and portable as possible have opened an infinite variety of body designs demonstrating the limitless imagination of the human mind. These instruments can use either an endpin or tripod to rest on the floor and can include some sort of knee rests.

Figure 3.19 shows three sides of one of the more imaginative examples of solid body cello designs. Figure 3.20 illustrates the flexibility taken advantage of by solid body cello makers. No holds barred!

Figure 3.19   Three Sides of a Solid Body Cello

Figure 3.20 Extraordinary Design Solid Body Cello

Electric Double Bass

Electric double basses are available in solid-body and hollow-body designs. Conventional acoustic double basses can also be amplified with the use of the pickups similar to those used on the smaller instruments. To review, these are the piezoelectric bridges (a form of electronic frequency generator), body pickups, a magnetic pickup attached to the bridge, body, or the end of or underside of the fingerboards, or a microphone. These pickups are connected with a cable to an amplifier using the same equipment as that used for the electric guitar.

Solid bodied basses that have no cavity in which the sound can resonate are entirely dependent on some form of amplification (Fig. 3.21). These instruments use magnetic and piezoelectric pickups to conduct the sound from the string to the amplifier and speakers.

Figure 3.21 Electric Double Basses

Electric double bass manufacturers also offer what might be referred to as a semi-solid body bass. This instrument has a cavity within the body similar to that of the solid-body cellos described previously. The cavity is of sufficient size to allow for some sound resonance which is then picked up by whatever amplification system is being used on that instrument.

Because of the low frequency of double bass notes, an equalizer, pre-amplifier with an amplifier, and low range speakers are needed to produce an acceptable sound. As is the case with the other three instruments of the violin family, one will find what might be described as extraordinarily creative designs for these basses.

A significant deviation some electric double basses take from the acoustic instrument occurs with the configuration of the fingerboard and bridge. Since the majority of electric basses are intended for use in pizzicato playing, some fingerboards and bridges lack the curve that is found in all other instruments of the violin family, both acoustic and electric.

That shape is necessary if one is to play arco (bowed) passages, for bowing on strings that are on a flat bridge would result in all strings being played at the same time. It is therefore necessary if one intends to play in venues that will include both pizzicato and arco techniques to select a traditional fingerboard and bridge configuration.

Summary

At this point in the evolution of the instruments of the violin family, the contemporary or modern iterations (those being the Baroque designs updated to accommodate the new strings) are most commonly used. The electric instruments, acoustic and solid-bodied, have reached what one might call an advancing state. Their current technology is still enjoying an ongoing effort to improve sound production while satisfying the physical and musical needs and passions of their players.

Baroque replicas, and in some cases actual Baroque instruments, are being used on a limited basis by those purists who wish to reproduce the original sound of Baroque music. Modified instruments, those redesigned to accommodate left handed players or resized to provide for the needs of younger students, will always be present on an as-needed basis.

The violin, viola, cello, and double bass in their contemporary form make up the largest and most versatile section of a traditional symphony orchestra. The three other versions of these four instruments, the Baroque, modified, and electric, play a significant role in every style of music and at all levels in music education.

The world continues to enjoy a love affair with what appears to be simple but beautiful wooden objects that produce a complexity of acoustical miracles, some of which have yet to be explained.

Chapter 4
Who Makes Them and
How They Are Made

The Industry

Understanding how an instrument is made gives the owner an insight into how it functions, how to play it, how to evaluate it, and how to select an upgrade instrument as the player advances.

Making violin family instruments differs from manufacturing other items in that even the most sophisticated computerized automated process still requires some hand assembly to complete the instrument. This type of instrument is not a product that can come off an assembly line completed and ready to use. Because of this singularity, string instrument making rather than manufacturing is more the term of art. Making high quality string instruments for professional use cannot be adapted to a large-scale production process. Every piece of wood used to make an instrument is unique in its structure, even when taken from the same tree. Therefore, the various parts of the instrument must be crafted in a way that will allow those differences to complement each other to form a unit capable of producing the desired sound. One procedure fits all cannot apply to making a *fine* string instrument.

On the other side of this spectrum, even the most inexpensive mass produced violin, viola, cello, or double bass must be hand finished if it is to function properly. Due to this phenomenon, the process of producing these instruments on a large scale has to be performed by trained specialists who make only one part of an instrument. These parts are then assembled by others and subsequently finished by still others to produce the final product.

In almost every industrialized country, one can find all the levels of string instrument production from individual luthiers with one-man shops to factories with multiple workers. The difference among them is found in the quality of the product they are turning out and the market they are serving. In the broadest sense, one can say that violins, violas, cellos, and double basses are made on three levels: custom made, handmade, and factory made.

Custom made instruments are fabricated by a luthier for a specific consumer. The process begins with the selection of the woods to be used. These may come from different parts of the world, for the same kind of wood grown in different climates will develop differently. Maple is used for the back, sides, and neck of the instrument, spruce for the top, and ebony or rosewood for the trim. Other woods and manmade products can be used as substitutes; however, maple, spruce, rosewood, and ebony have been found to be the most effective materials for producing a good instrument.

The next step in the process is designing the instrument. Generally, a copy of the designs of the masters, i.e., Stradivari, Guarneri, Amati, etc., is followed, but there can also be variations on those or some other pattern which is uniquely the luthier's design.

When the wood and design patterns are decided upon, the luthier carves, shapes, and molds the various parts to the specifications of the design selected. The instrument is then assembled, stained, varnished, and hand rubbed. These few simple sentences represent a minimum of at least 25 steps, each requiring hours and in some cases days to complete. After this series is completed, the luthier fits the instrument with pegs, tailpiece, bridge, strings, and a chinrest. This caliber of instrument is often made to order for a specific individual but can also be made by a luthier who will then find buyers for them.

The process for fabricating handmade string instruments follows the same procedure as that used for custom made instruments; however, handmade instruments can be made by more than one luthier within a shop. The fabrication of each part may be assigned to different individuals who specialize in making that part. The handmade parts are then assembled by still another maker and setup by yet another. The instrument is still handmade but by more than one pair of hands.

Factories which make musical instruments on a large scale have been developing in China over the past twenty years so that now these factories and shops make seventy percent of the world's non-fretted string instruments. China's string instrument industry has become a challenge to the traditional string instrument producing countries such as Italy, Germany, and France.

Donggaocun, a suburb of Beijing, China, and Xiqiao, a town in southeast China, claim to produce thirty percent of the world's supply of violins, violas, cellos, and double basses. Donggaocun, which boasts of having 9 factories and 150 smaller individual workshops, claims to have produced as many as 250,000 string instruments a year, most of which are sold to the U.S., U.K., and Germany. These factories have grown from originally producing some very poor to mediocre products to what are now considered to be excellent quality instruments on many levels.

The volume of production in China has been achieved through a system of training which uses master craftsmen as mentors. These teachers hold seminars, competitions, and reward excellence both monetarily and with prestigious recognition for achievement. The workers in the factories are trained in the production of a specific part of an instrument. Each worker concentrates on machine making that single piece in large quantities. All parts of the instrument are then assembled at a final point in the process. The concept here is that if a worker makes only violin scrolls, he or she is more likely to refine that art than one attempting to make many parts of the instrument.

The preparation for becoming a luthier in China begins in high school and progresses over an eleven-year period to include a four-year university program followed by three years on the master's level. Throughout these years, the students study the physics of sound and other sciences, along with an intense focus on learning to evaluate the attributes of the raw materials to be used. All of this technological learning is reinforced under the guidance and supervision of the master luthiers associated with an apprentice program.

Factory made violins can also be produced with parts that are made in large quantities by automated machines. The individual parts are punched out on dies or carved by computer-guided lathes and other types of woodworking machines. The parts are then assembled and setup with the fittings by hand. If properly made with reasonably good material, factory made instruments do serve as a practical source of instruments for beginning students.

Whether custom made, handmade, or factory made, it must be understood that the final product is as good as the raw materials used and the expertise of those implementing the process. High quality woods used in an excellent factory can turn out a better instrument than one handmade with lesser quality raw materials and a less skilled luthier. So, the question to ask is, "What is the difference and how do I select an instrument?"

Careful examination of the final product and evaluating the workmanship and quality of the materials used are the first steps to noting the difference among instruments. The final and most important test is in the playing. If it sounds the way you want it to sound, is well made from high quality material and in good condition, it will most likely be an instrument worthy of consideration. Chapter 6 describes in detail the process for selecting an instrument.

The Process

The four instruments of the violin family are all constructed using very similar processes. Because the violin is the most standardized of the four in both size and structure, it will be used as the model for the instrument making process. The reader will bear in mind that the description to follow represents the fundamental processes used to construct all of the four instruments in the violin family. Using these basic procedures, an individual maker or factory will modify each step to suit specific artistic and acoustical goals.

A violin maker (luthier) is a unique kind of artisan who must possess a combination of talents that one would not immediately associate with making a musical instrument. A luthier must be an historian, for instruments of the violin family are constructed on patterns made centuries ago by the great masters who started the process, an architect able to design the instrument to be built, a skilled wood carver capable of shaping wood to within a millimeter of the design requirement, a structural engineer who can devise the process needed to assemble the instrument parts, a skilled craftsman with the ability to execute the assembly process, an acoustician with the musical instincts to define and discern some of the most complex sounds on the basis of principles of physics, an artist who will be able to complete and adjust the final product with a finish that transcends that of even the greatest wooden sculpture, and all with a tenacity that will settle for nothing but perfection.

How an Instrument Is Made

Following are the basic steps a luthier will use to make a non-fretted string instrument. The presentation is intended to give an overview of the process. The reader must bear in mind that luthiers are artists and, as such, will modify these basic processes to suit their originality and creativity.

Step 1 – Establishing the Pattern

The luthier will decide on the basic model and design to be used. This design could resemble any one of the styles of the masters with whatever modifications are appropriate for this new instrument's intended role in the music world. An example of a choice might be a Stradivari model from a particular period in his long career, or an Amati, Guarneri, or any of the many different iterations of the instruments that were built during the evolution of the subject instrument.

Step 2 – Selecting the Material

Selecting the various woods to be used is perhaps the most challenging undertaking the luthier faces, for the woods will be the heart and soul of the instrument, the parents of the sounds to be heard. The selection must be implemented with wisdom, skill, experience, intuition, and artistry. As already stated, the woods used to make the major parts of a violin are usually spruce for the top, maple for the sides, back, and neck, and ebony or rosewood for the fingerboard, pegs, and trim. Small, inner parts called blocks and linings (to be defined later) are often made of willow.

The wood selection process can consist of anything from the luthier's own intuition to a scientific evaluation of the acoustical properties of a particular piece of wood. The entire topic is subject to opinion, calculation, and speculation, combining both empirical and anecdotal procedures. Suffice to say that the selection process can have as many variants as there are luthiers.

Step 3 – Cutting the Wood

(Repeated from chapter 2 for the convenience of the reader)

There are two ways in which wood can be cut to make the upper and lower plates (top and back) of the violin. If the maker intends to construct an instrument with a two piece back plate, the wood is cut into a triangular shaped block which is then cut vertically down the middle to form two triangles (Fig. 4.1).

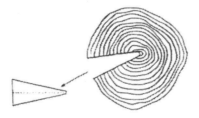

Figure 4.1   V- Shape Wood Cut

The second possibility is to cut a layer of wood that will produce a one piece plate. This method eliminates the seam from the middle of the plate (Fig. 4.2). The disadvantage of this method is the likelihood that a one piece slab of wood, because of the span of the size required, will have a variation in grain as the cut progresses. It is most desirable to maintain a uniform grain in the production of these plates. The triangle cut maintains this uniformity because the cuts are taken from a smaller portion of the overall slab of wood.

Figure 4.2   Cross Cut Wood Cut

Step 4 – Joining the Cuts

If the original cut is V shaped, the two pieces are "book matched," joined together with hide glue, a water soluble product made from animal connective tissue. The matched pieces are placed in a jig to dry and form one plate (Fig. 4.3). This type of cut is used to increase the likelihood of achieving a symmetrical wood grain pattern.

Figure 4.3 Joining the Cuts

When the glue is dry, the two pieces that have become one are removed from the jig and a pattern for the outline of the instrument's back is traced on to that piece (Fig. 4.4).

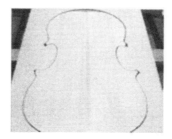

Figure 4.4 Outline

The wood is then cut with a band saw following the outline while leaving some additional material to allow for future adjustments (Fig. 4.5).

Figure 4.5 Back First Cut

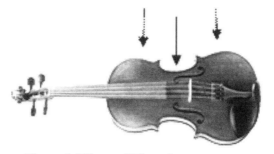

Figure 4.6 Upper, "C", and Lower Bouts

N.B. Violin family instrument terminology uses the term "bout" to identify the upper, middle, and lower thirds of an instrument. The upper bout and lower bout are the two large upper and lower thirds of the instrument. The center narrow section is called the "C" bout (Fig. 4.6).

Step 5 – The Mold

The first step in assembling the parts of the instrument occurs when the luthier prepares a wooden form called a mold. It can be made with a variety of interior structures designed to hold the clamps needed in the building process. The exterior of the molds are all shaped to the size and form of the intended instrument. The mold is the foundation on which the first parts of the instrument will be assembled. Figure 4.7 shows two types of molds, both with the same exterior shape but each with a different interior clamp-holding design.

With the mold in place, six wooden blocks, usually of a soft wood such as willow, poplar, or spruce, are prepared and placed on the mold to act as anchors for the instrument's sides or ribs. One (corner) block is placed in each of the four corners of the C bouts and a fifth and sixth (end) block are placed at the upper and lower end of the mold (Fig. 4.7).

Figure 4.7 Mold

Step 6 – The Ribs

The ribs or sides of an instrument are thin strips of maple usually about 1.2 mm thick and 35 mm wide. To create the ribs, the luthier moistens the wood strips to increase their flexibility and then heats and bends them to the desired shape. An electric heating device called a bending iron is commonly used to achieve this end. Another method of heating and moistening ribs uses steam. When using this process both moistening take place simultaneously, probably easier than using a bending iron. Figure 4.8 illustrates heated ribs placed around a mold. Attention is given to matching the grain of ribs for esthetic reasons.

Figure 4.8 Forming the Ribs

Step 7 - The Linings

After the ribs have been glued to the blocks and the glue is dry, thin strips of wood called linings are dry fitted and then glued around the edge of the ribs. The dry fitting process is used to ensure that the linings fit perfectly before the glue is applied. The linings support the ribs after they are removed from the mold (Fig. 4.9).

Figure 4.9 Lining

Step 8 – Carving the Plates

In step 4, the upper and lower plates, (top and back) were rough cut. These now must be carved into the configuration prescribed by the original instrument plan. Master luthier Scott Hershey, pictured above, claims he is "carving away everything that's not a violin." An assortment of the violin

violin maker's chisels, gouges, and knives specifically designed for this task along with any implements that are proprietary to the luthier are used to perform this complex process.

It is at this point that the luthier's expertise is challenged because the top and back of the instrument are the two major components forming the resonating chamber that will amplify and either enhance or not enhance the final sounds produced on this instrument. The carving process is arduous, tedious, challenging, and demanding of the highest degree of artistic proficiency if the final product is to be successful in producing beautiful sounds (Fig. 4.10).

Figure 4.10 Carving Process

Step 9 – Purfling

Purfling is a thin, double strip of wood that is inlaid into the edge of the top and back of the instrument. This may appear to be ornamental but, in fact, it serves two purposes. Structurally, purfling acts as reinforcement for the edges of the instrument preventing any severe damage from occurring to the upper and lower plates, should the edge suffer a blow. Acoustically, the groove that is cut into the plates acts as an interruption to the vibrations that are traveling through the wood. These interruptions provide the luthier with an opportunity to control to some degree the area of vibration and in so doing, modify the instrument's sound.

Figure 4.11 shows a luthier marking the groove (A), cutting the groove (B), and the finished product with the purfling installed (C). Purfling is one of the many points on an instrument where the craftsmanship of a luthier is demonstrated by the accuracy with which the corners of the purfling are matched.

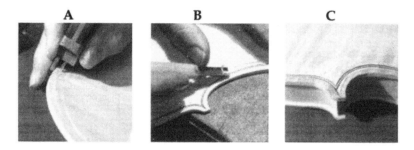

Figure 4.11 Installing Purfling

Step 10 – Tuning the Plates

To tune a top or bottom plate, it must be set into a vibrating mode. This can be accomplished manually by tapping on the plate or electronically by generating a sympathetic vibration. To tune a plate using an electronic procedure, a tone generator, amplifier with volume control, and a speaker, are set to produce sounds of different amplitudes and frequencies. A gigue is used to hold a plate suspended above the speaker. With the inside of the plate facing up and suspended over the speaker, glitter is sprinkled over the plate's surface. The sound apparatus is then activated, producing pitches of different frequencies at high amplitudes. These sounds set the plate into motion through sympathetic vibration. As the plate vibrates, the glitter migrates forming various patterns called Chladni (the father of acoustics) patterns which show the nodes, the points where there is no vibration and antinodes, the points of significant vibration (Fig. 4.12). It is through this testing that the luthier decides the location on the plates where material should be removed to produce the tone desired.

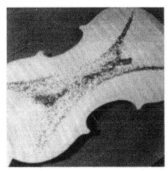

Figure 4.12 Tuning the Plates

Using the tapping method, the luthier gingerly holds a plate between the thumb and forefinger and with the other hand taps on the plate in various locations. The resulting sounds are called "tap-tones." These are actual pitches that indicate to the experienced luthier how much material should be shaved from the various areas of the plate in order to achieve the desired tonal result. The differential of the tap-tones found on a plate can be as much as an octave. It is not uncommon for a luthier to use both the electronic (scientific) and tapping (artistic) methods to achieve the best possible results.

Step 11 –"F" Holes

"F" holes or sound holes are a crucial part of the sound producing system of all violin family instruments (Fig. 4.13).

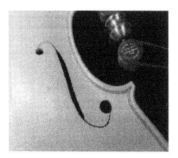

Figure 4.13 Finished "f" Holes

The manner in which these tone holes are shaped, their size, and relationship to each other play an important role in the final tone quality and sound projection of an instrument. With proper understanding and the skill to implement that understanding, the luthier has the opportunity to finesse the sound of the instrument being constructed. Cutting the "f" holes is a very delicate process (Fig. 4.14). A pattern is designed based on a calculation of the size, shape, and distance of the holes from each other needed to produce the intended sound. A notch is added in the mid-point of each side as a guide to placing the bridge at a future time.

"F" holes must be at least as large as is necessary to allow a sound post to pass through later in the process. Once the luthier decides on the exact size and shape to be used, the instrument's upper plate is marked with that shape. Pilot holes are then drilled in strategic places in the pattern and a jeweler's saw is used for the preliminary cuts. These are followed by cuts made with a series of very sharp knives selected by the luthier to finish the job.

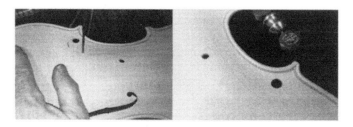

Figure 4.14 Cutting the "F" Holes

Step 12 - The Bass Bar

At this point, with the top, back, and sides near completion, the luthier must make the bass bar, a strip of wood attached to the underside of the top plate. This strip reinforces the plate while distributing the lower pitches throughout the area. The bass bar is first rough cut (Fig. 4.15) and then shaped and modified as needed to ultimately fulfill its role.

Figure 4.15 Shaping the Bass Bar

The bass bar is then glued in place (Fig. 4.16).

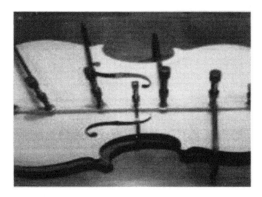

Figure 4.16 Gluing the Bass Bar

When the glue is dry, the clamps are removed and the luthier proceeds to do another plate tuning (Fig. 4.17). This step is necessary to modify any changes the addition of the bass bar may have made in the top plate's response to vibration.

Figure 4.17 Re-tuning the Plate

Step 13 – The Neck

The neck and scroll are carved from one piece of hard flamed maple that will closely match the flaming of the back plate of the instrument. Using a template, an outline is drawn on a perfectly planed wood block. A coping saw or band saw is used to remove the excess wood that surrounds the outline (Fig. 4.18).

 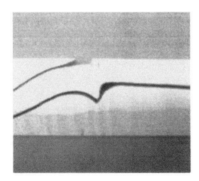

Figure 4.18 Cutting the Neck

The location for the peg holes is then marked on the cutout (Fig. 4.19).

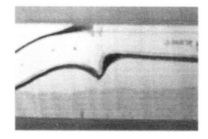

Figure 4.19 Marking the Peg Holes

The peg box is outlined and the inside and outside dimensions of the scroll are traced using pre-cut patterns (Fig. 4.20).

Figure 4.20 Outlining the Peg Box

When those steps are completed, sharp knives and files are used to shape the neck (Fig. 4.21).

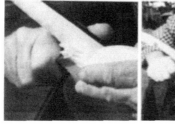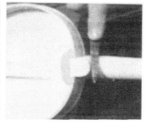

Figure 4.21 Shaping the Neck

Step 14 – Peg Holes

Pilot peg holes are drilled into what is still a solid block (Fig. 22). They will be refined at a later time in the process.

Figure 4.22 Drilling the Peg Holes

The accuracy with which the peg holes are cut will determine how efficiently the pegs do their job. Properly fitted pegs will move easily to facilitate tuning the strings and will hold them in place without slipping after they are tuned.

Step 15 – The Scroll

The scroll on a handmade instrument is often a form of trademark or signature for the one who carves it. This is an opportunity for the luthier to demonstrate his/her craftsmanship. It is not uncommon for luthiers to show their artisanship by personalizing their scroll or replacing the traditional scroll with a carved head of a person or animal.

The reader may recall that the outline of the scroll was scribed on the solid neck block of wood illustrated in Figure 4.17. Using that pattern as a guide, multiple back saw cuts are made on those markings to remove the excess wood (Fig. 4.23).

Figure 4.23 Cutting the Scroll

It is at this point that the luthier must shift to sculptor to achieve a signature final product. One technique used to ensure symmetry is to carve both sides of the scroll simultaneously alternating back and forth to constantly check for balance. Gauges, scrapers, and other individualized tools are used to carve the remainder of the scroll to the final shape (Fig. 4.24).

Figure 4.24 Three Stages of Carving the Scroll

Step 16 - The Peg Box

The peg box that was outlined previously in Figure 4.19 is carved next. It must be accurately sized and shaped since that will be the space in which the pegs with wound strings will reside.

The peg box cheeks (sides) are marked on the block and then the luthier uses a drill to remove a significant portion of the wood (Fig. 4.25).

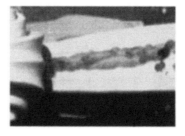

Figure 4.25 Starting the Peg Box

When a sufficient amount of excess wood is removed, the luthier switches to a series of sharp carving tools such as chisels and gouges to carve out the remaining wood forming the final peg box shape and dimensions (Fig. 4.26).

Figure 4.26 Carving the Peg Box

The final product pictured in Figure 4.27 is a smooth, well-proportioned properly sized peg box. This is part of the neck which is now ready to be attached to the body of the instrument.

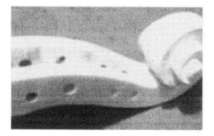

Figure 4.27 Finishing the Peg Box

Step 17 – Fitting the Neck to the Body

The important issue at this juncture is aligning the neck perfectly with the instrument in preparation for the placement of the fingerboard. The slightest deviation from true will render the instrument close to useless. It is along this path that the strings will travel from the peg box over the fingerboard and the bridge to end at the tailpiece. With the upper plate in place and a mortis (opening) cut into the top block to fit the base of the neck, it is glued in place
Fig. 4.28)

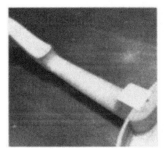
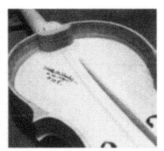

Figure 4.28 Attaching the Neck

With the neck in place and the glue dry, the back plate is next in line to be glued on to the ribs (Fig. 4.29).

Figure 4.29 Attaching the Back Plate

Step 18 - The Setup

To complete the instrument before varnishing, a fingerboard (Fig. 4.30A), nut (Fig. 4.30B), and saddle (Fig. 4.30C) are cut, finished and glued in place.

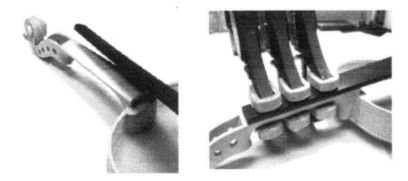

Figure 4.30A Gluing the Fingerboard

Figure 4.30B Fitting the Nut

Figure 4.30C Fitting the Saddle

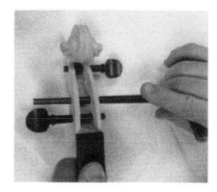

Figure 4.31A Reaming the Peg Holes

The pegs are shaved to fit those holes (Fig. 4.31B).

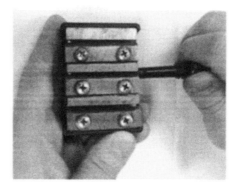

Figure 4.31B Shaving the Pegs

The pegs are then installed in the peg box (Fig. 4.31C)

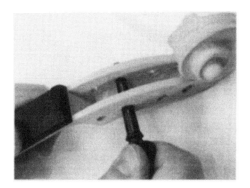

Figure 4.31C Installing the Pegs

The bridge is cut (Fig. 4.32A) and it and the sound post (Fig 4.32B) are fitted.

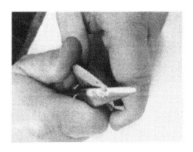

Figure 4.32A	**Figure 4.32B**
Cutting the Bridge	**Setting the Sound Post**

An end button (Fig. 4.33A), tailpiece (Fig. 4.33B), and chin rest (Fig. 4.33C) are fitted and the instrument is ready to be strung and tried for sound in the white before varnishing.

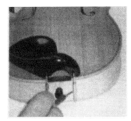

Figure 4.33A	**Figure 4.33B**	**Figure4.33C**
Tailpiece	**End Button**	**Chin Rest**

The instrument has now been setup "in the white" (Fig 4.34) (without a finish) for the first trial playing. At this time the luthier will make any adjustments needed to refine and maximize the sound produced by this new instrument.

Figure 4.34 Setup in the White

Step 19 - The Finish N.B. *The term "finish" in this section will refer to the coating applied to the raw wood of an instrument after its construction is complete.*

The process and material used to apply a finish to an instrument is a topic that could justifiably be considered one of the most controversial in the music industry. Beginning with the preparation of a "white" instrument, that being one that is complete except for the finish, questions arise as to what preparatory steps, follow-up procedures, and material are to be used? Countless opinions are proffered on all aspects of how this should be accomplished and these are discussed and argued ad infinitum. There are as many opinions as there are luthiers with the addition of scientists, chemists, physicists, and historians. Because of this controversy, the following description of how a violin family instrument is finished will be restricted to the basic fundamental steps used by all practitioners who then modify and expand the process in whatever way suits their opinions and abilities.

The five steps generally used to finish an instrument include a preparation of the finish to receive the various coatings, a ground which is the application of some sort of base to the raw wood, the addition of color to the wood, a final application of some sort of protective coating, and a polishing process of choice.

Preparation

To prepare the raw wood, the luthier *may* start by wetting the surface to raise the grain. Wetting causes swelling of the wood cells allowing the luthier to modify the wood grain to whatever degree desired. The modification is achieved by sanding, scraping, or a combination of both until the preferred effect is achieved. Other proprietary methods may also be used at the discretion of the luthier.

Ground Layer or Coat

Ground or ground coat is the term used for the application of a sealing agent that will prepare raw wood to receive color and a finishing product. Ground can consist of various oils or propolis, a waxy substance taken from the inside of a beehive. These products will fill the pores in the wood and cover any blemishes that may have resulted in the fabrication process. The objective is to have a smooth surface on which to proceed with the finishing process.

Applying a ground is also considered by some to be one of the steps that can be taken to alter the sound of an instrument by rebalancing the ratio of high to low frequencies. Although there is no empirical evidence to validate this theory, there is some logic to the concept that altering the cell structure of an instrument could in some way modify its ability to vibrate and produce different sounds (Fig. 4.35).

Figure 4.35 Applying the Ground

Color

Applying color is totally subjective in both the color choice and the technique used in the application. There are innumerable combinations of coloring pigments available in every conceivable form on the commercial market. Additionally, many luthiers are inclined to use their own proprietary formulae. The application processes share the same multitude of individual choices ranging from being wiped on with a cloth to sprays and all the brushing and direct hand application techniques imaginable.

Finishing Coat

Again, individual choice reigns. Varnishing anything is no easy task. Applying varnish to a musical instrument so that it will look good, vibrate freely to amplify sound, and survive direct handling throughout its entire life requires an expert. Whatever product used, the almost universally agreed upon aphorism is to keep it light. Several coats interspersed with a fine sanding usually yields the best results because a heavier application will most likely mute sound production.

When the application is thoroughly cured, the luthier might finesse the finish with a hand polishing using any combination of oils, bees' wax, pumice, rotten stone and turpentine, or anything else s/he may feel will best complete the job (Fig. 4.36).

Figure 4.36 Finessing the Finish

Figure 4.37 The Finished Product

Summary

And so another handmade instrument is born. With proper care it can live for centuries. In the hands of professionals it will provide the world with millions of notes which, when properly combined, will become music. Think back to that first individual who plucked the string that made the sound that began the process that led to the violin, viola, cello, and double bass. What a wonder. Thank you, luthiers of the world, both past and present for your contributions to humankind's musical joy.

How a Bow Is Made

Preface

When one evaluates an instrument from the violin family, the focus is most often on the instrument with much less attention given to the bow that will be used to play that instrument. This is tantamount to evaluating a car without paying attention to the engine, for the bow is, in effect, the engine that drives the instrument. Good instrument + bad bow = bad sound. This is so much the case that instrumentalists at the highest level in the profession spend countless hours seeking the bow that is best suited to their instrument. Often they will have a particular archetier (bow maker) whom they call their own to assist in obtaining the bow that will satisfy their needs.

Bow making is an art form and, as such, the process is subject to as many variations as there are bow makers. The following is a description of the basic process one follows to make a bow. From these generally accepted procedures, individual makers will add their own signature to each step. To the layman, the bow appears to be simply a stick with hair attached to it. In fact, it is constructed of between thirteen and fifteen parts which, in order to be effective, must be fabricated with meticulous care. The most apparent parts of the bow are the stick, hair, and frog. Not easily visible are the inside workings that keep it all together.

The Materials

The materials needed to make a bow consist of wood for the stick, usually Pernambuco with a straight, dense gain, ebony for the frog, a metal of choice, often silver, nickel silver, or gold for the metal fittings, a hard wood dowel for the adjustor screw barrel, a sheet of mother of pearl or abalone for the slides, a few hardwood plugs and wedges, and a hank of horsehair. For less expensive bows, all of these materials can be substituted with almost anything from lesser quality woods to fiberglass and plastic.

The Stick

The first step in the fabrication process is the selection of the wood to be used for the stick. The best bows are usually made with Pernambuco. This wood is cut with a saw into a long strip with no definitive shape called a straight blank. The blank is then roughly formed into an octagonal shape. If the final product is to have a rounded stick, the cutting down of the octagonal edges is performed toward the end of the process. More on that later. It is during this process that the archetier checks for defects or interruptions in the grain which can take the form of a knot, worm hole, or defect of any kind. Figure 4.38 illustrates an archetier planning the octagonal facets on a bow blank.

Figure 4.38 Planing the Bow Stick

The Head or Tip

After the stick is formed, the bow maker carves the head of the bow. A bone or ivory tip is glued in place; the tip is roughed out using a knife and then refined with an assortment of files (Fig. 4.39).

Figure 4.39 Refining the Tip

When shaping the head is completed, a mortise (opening) is cut into its base (Fig. 4.40).

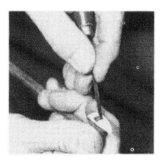

Figure 4.40 Cutting the Mortise

This is in preparation for accepting the hair (Fig. 4.41).

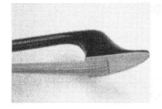

Figure 4.41 The Hair in Place

On the other end of the stick it will be necessary to cut a mortise to accommodate the eyelet part of the frog (Fig. 4.42). A detailed description of these parts will follow in the frog-making section.

Figure 4.42 The Frog Mortise

After the mortise is cut, a hole is drilled from the end of the stick to the mortise to accommodate the adjustor screw barrel part of the frog (Fig 4.43).

Figure 4.43 Drilling the Stick

To reinforce the stick at that point, a hardwood dowel is installed in the hole and then another hole is drilled into that dowel in which the adjuster screw (Fig. 4.44) will travel without damaging the stick itself.

Figure 4.44 Adjuster Screw

Creating the Camber

When the stick is shaped reasonably close to that which will be the final product, it is time to create the camber or arc. To do this the archetier heats the stick using a soft flame such as that from an alcohol lamp. (Fig. 4.45). When the stick has reached the proper temperature and displays sufficient flexibility, it is pressed against a form in a succession of moves until the required camber is achieved. The stick is then cooled to retain the arc that was formed.

Figure 4.45 Creating the Camber

The Frog

The frog is the only movable mechanism on the bow. This ebony block to which the bow hair is connected requires the greatest number of steps in the bow making process. The bow maker begins shaping a blank piece of ebony (Fig. 4.46) into a trapezoid which will ultimately be several millimeters wider on the bottom than the top. The sides are then shaped to a slightly concave configuration.

Figure 4.46 Blank Ebony Blocks

The front of the frog will then be shaped into a "U" which faces the tip of the bow (Fig 4.47). The lower leg of the "U" is carved into a half-round.

Figure 4.47 "U" Shape on Frog

It is at this point that the hair will enter the frog and ultimately be held in a mortise cut out of the frog. Figure 4.48 shows a blank frog with an unfinished mortise.

Figure 4.48 Unfinished Mortise

Figure 4.49 shows a frog with a mortise ready to accept hair.

Figure 4.49 Mortise Ready

Figure 4.50 shows a frog with the hair installed. Note the metal half round band at the end of the frog. This is called a ferrule (Fig. 4.51).

Figure 4.50 Hair Installed

Figure 4.51 Ferrule

On the underside of the frog behind the ferrule is a mother of pearl slide which covers the mortise and holds the hair in place (Fig. 4.52A). Continuing from that slide is a silver plate which travels up the back of the frog to its top (Fig. 4.52B). On either side of the frog a mother of pearl eye is inlaid solely for decorative purposes (Fig. 4.52C).

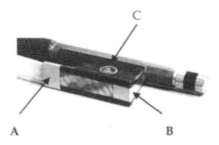

Figure 4.52 External Frog Parts

Fitting the Frog

The top of the frog is configured to fit the stick. To reinforce the frog and ease its sliding back and forth on the stick, a strip of metal called an underslide is usually made of nickel silver and is shaped with facets to match those of the stick. This slide is placed on the top of the frog to help support it and prevent cracking (Fig. 4.53).

Figure 4.53 Underslide

In fitting the frog to the stick, the objective will be to have the frog fit securely with no wobble yet move easily back and forth when the bow hair is loosened or tightened. The mechanism that tightens and loosens the bow hair consists of a screw and eyelet with a button on the end of the screw. The eyelet (Fig. 4.54A) is installed into the top of the frog through the metal underslide and receives the screw (Fig. 4.54B) that will move the frog. The button at the end of the screw (Fig. 4.54C) is octagonal to match the shape of the bow stick and is made in three sections with a mother of pearl dot at its end for decorative proposes.

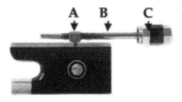

Figure 4.54 Screw and Eyelet

The Bow Grip

Just forward of the frog on the stick is a wrapping or bow grip which can be made of almost any material that can be wrapped around a stick. Most commonly used are whalebone, silver, leather, or rubber (Fig. 4.55).

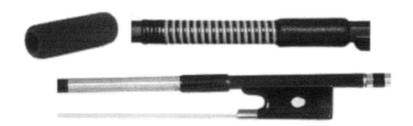

Figure 4.55 Bow Grips

Completing the Stick

Thus far in the bow making process, the archetier, starting with a "blank" strip of wood for the stick, carved and shaped it, built a frog to fit the stick, carved the tip, and cut a mortise into that tip to receive the hair.

Next, refining the shape of the stick takes place. The goal will be to have the bow taper from the tip to the button that controls the movement of the frog so that the differential is about three millimeters. When that process is completed, the archetier will determine if the flexibility of the stick is acceptable. If it is too stiff, it can be tempered by planing down the octagon shape to sixteen facets or making the final product round. Throughout this entire process, the archetier will periodically sight the bow to ensure that it is maintaining a true course (Fig. 4.56).

Figure 4.56 Sighting the Bow

When all the balancing and shaping is complete, the final step would be to apply color if desired and then burnish and French polish the wood to achieve a finished product. When all the parts are finished, it is time to install horsehair on the bow stick.

Hairing the Bow

Use diagram 4.57 as a guide. To hair a bow, a hank of horse hair (A) is selected and combed so that all hairs are parallel to each other. The end of the hank is then tied and wedged securely into a box-shaped cutout (mortise) at the tip of the bow (B). The hair is held in place by a wooden, wedge-shaped plug (C) that is accurately cut to exactly fit the space remaining in the cutout box. This plug holds the hair in place.

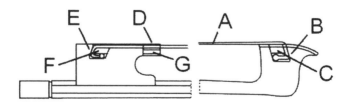

Figure 4.57 Bow Hair Diagram

A ferrule, metal band (D) is inserted over the hair which is carefully drawn along the bow, tied at the end, and inserted into a similar box-shaped cutout in the frog (E). Again, a wooden wedge-shaped plug is placed into the box (F) to secure the hair in place. A slide and another wooden wedge are inserted between the ferrule and the frog (G) to help distribute the hairs equally and laterally and to keep them in place.

Summary

A bow is the driving force responsible for the sound that instrument produces. As such, it is essential that the archetier execute the bow-making process with the expertise necessary to ensure that, when coupled with an instrument, the combination will produce a sound fully representative of the instrument's potential. The quality of the wood selected, how it is formed into a well-balanced stick with adequate resilience, proper camber, and correct weight for its intended use are only some of the challenges that confront master bow makers. These individuals might well be among the unsung heroes of the non-fretted string instrument world.

Chapter 5
How to Choose and Buy
A String Instrument

Choosing a string instrument to buy is a challenge for even the most astute experienced musician. Because instruments in the violin family are made of wood, a reactive substance, and have an architecture that is conducive to extraordinary individuality, each of these instruments is its own person.

One can play six trumpets of the same brand and model in succession and find each with some difference but generally they will all respond in like manner. This will be the case with most items fabricated of manmade material. It is possible to make a substance such as fiberglass in large quantities that will have a consistent basic structure. Fiberglass bows of the same model and manufacturer are generally very much the same. Natural wood does not share that characteristic. Each piece of wood is unique and so each instrument made from a piece of wood has its own individuality. The search for an instrument then becomes a matter of having exposure to as many instruments of the kind being sought as possible. This chapter will help direct the reader in the process of finding an instrument that will satisfy most of the requirements needed for an enjoyable ownership experience.

Musical instruments can be bought for almost any price and any quality. When searching for an instrument to purchase, the process should include an understanding of what qualities to look for and how to recognize them. Additionally, a realistic awareness of how likely one's expectations can be fulfilled within the decided price range must be part of the buyer's preparation prior to beginning the search. The following are some hints on how to proceed.

1. The Price

Determine a price range with a span of about $300. e.g., 100-400, 500-800, 900-1200, etc. Keep in mind that although it is possible to buy a violin or viola for one hundred dollars, it will more than likely be worthless. Also, one must accept the fact that a one hundred dollar cello or double bass of any musical value does not exist.

2. Old vs. New

Ask to see both new and older instruments in the selected price range. As is the case with any art form, and these instruments certainly can be considered a form of art, there are many theories and opinions on whether new or old is the better choice. The more commonly held opinions are as follows:

A bad new or bad old string instrument will always be bad so avoid those. You will learn how to do so in the following pages.

A good new instrument, if properly cared for, will become a better instrument as it is played and the wood ages.

An old good string instrument, depending on its age, will probably not improve as much as a new one, since it has most likely already done so.

What to do? Try them all and try to find the instrument you love.

3. Take a Good Look

Perform a visual inspection of the instruments offered in your chosen price range. Check the interior and exterior for cracks, open seams, chips, dents, or scratches and any evidence of repair of any kind. Keep in mind that chips dents or scratches do not necessarily affect the performance of an instrument but they do affect the value.

Inside - A look inside what is offered as an old instrument will show if, in fact, it really is old. Luthiers are very skilled at making the exterior of a new instrument look old but the inside will tell the story. If the wood on the inside of the instrument is light in color, new, and fresh in appearance, it is likely to be new. Old instruments are old both inside and out. It is more difficult for a luthier to age the inside of an instrument than the outside.

Repairs - A properly repaired crack or re-glued seam is acceptable; however, a repaired crack can lower the value of an instrument. The operative word here is properly. A proper crack repair should be difficult to spot and almost, if not completely smooth to the touch. Close your eyes and pass your finger across the repaired crack. You should feel almost no evidence of a repair.

The next step will be to examine the neck and fingerboard of the instrument. The neck should be free of cracks and smooth to the touch on the underside. This portion of the instrument is generally not finished as is the body but rather oiled and hand rubbed in order to provide a smooth surface for the player's hand to slide up and down the various positions.

In some better quality older instruments, one may see a splice where the neck joins the body. The reader will remember from chapter 1 that the projection (angle) of the neck on an older violin was flatter and the neck shorter. On an old good instrument, the splice may be an indication of the neck angle correction or even of the neck being replaced to accommodate contemporary strings. This can be a good indication that the instrument was considered by someone to be worthy of this type of alteration. Unfortunately, this splice is sometimes put on a newer instrument to deceive the buyer into thinking it is an old instrument of good quality.

Warping - Holding the instrument in such a position as to be able to look down the fingerboard from the peg box toward the bridge, one must check to be sure that the fingerboard is smooth, true, and not warped. If there is any buzzing when a string is plucked or bowed, that is an indication of a possibly warped fingerboard or improperly fitted nut. Check it out before you proceed. The space between the string and fingerboard at the point of the nut should be sufficient to allow the string to vibrate easily but not so high as to be uncomfortable for the player.

The Set-up - The term "set up" refers to the manner in which the strings rest on the nut at the top of the fingerboard and travel down the fingerboard and over the bridge to be connected to the tailpiece. Although it is possible to present some measurements for general reference, the final dimensions are peculiar to each instrument. A proper set up will have a bridge that is arched to allow the four strings to be easily bowed individually or in conjunction with each other when playing double stops. The slots in which the strings are placed on the bridge should be only as deep as is necessary to prevent the strings from moving horizontally. To achieve optimum sound, the bridge should be positioned so that the feet are in direct alignment with the notches visible in the center of the inside of the F holes.

The Bridge - When viewing an instrument's bridge from its side, one should insure that the side of the bridge facing the tail piece is flat and at a perfect 90 degree angle from the top of the instrument (Fig 5.1A) and that the fingerboard side of the bridge is graduated to a smaller thickness toward its top (Fig 5.1B). The illusion is that the bridge appears to be leaning toward the tailpiece. This configuration is intended to compensate for the tendency of a bridge to warp in the direction of the fingerboard as a result of the strings being pulled toward the fingerboard when tuning.

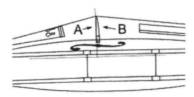

Figure 5.1 Viewing the Bridge

After checking to see that the bridge is properly centered between the two notches on the sides of the "f" holes, look down the fingerboard from the peg box again to check the alignment of the strings. They should travel in a direct line from the peg box over the nut, over the fingerboard, over the bridge and to the tailpiece.

The Pegs - Pegs on a violin, viola, and cello hold the strings in tune and must be properly installed if they are to work effectively. They must turn smoothly and remain firmly in place when the instrument is tuned. The pegs should be installed so that the ears extend a comfortable distance out from the peg box and the opposite end of the peg is flush with the outside of the peg box. The peg ends should not protrude from the peg box.

The hole in the peg through which the string is threaded should be close to the narrow end of the peg. This is necessary to allow the string to wind around the peg smoothly and progress concentrically away from the hole toward the center of the peg. Although other woods and manmade products are sometimes used, pegs are most often made of rosewood or ebony. It is essential that the pegs be made of a hard wood if they are to stay in place.

As stated above, the space between the string and the fingerboard at the nut should be enough to allow the string to vibrate easily and yet not so great as to be uncomfortable for the player. If the slot in the nut is too deep, the open string will buzz. If the nut is too high, the player will feel it as being uncomfortable when depressing a string.

The Top - A comparison of several instruments will show some variation in the arch or bulge of the center of the top as compared to its sides. It is generally believed that instruments with higher arches tend to produce a more aggressive or nasal tone as compared with those with flatter arching. Often, instruments with the higher arch are lower in price than a comparable instrument with a lower arch. Additionally, those older, higher arched instruments have increased in value less than that of their flatter counterparts. That being said, the final choice should still be the instrument which satisfies most of the requirements of the player.

The Woods - Look beyond the finish of the instrument into the wood grain. A variety of woods are used in making string instruments. For an instrument to perform properly, its different parts require different strengths and resonance responses to make up the whole sound-producing device. Although there are exceptions, traditionally spruce is used for the top, the blocks, and the linings. Maple is used for the sides, back, neck, and scroll, and ebony for the pegs, fingerboard, tailpiece, and end button. Woods other than spruce maple and ebony can be used. The most common substitute is boxwood in place of ebony parts. For the less expensive instruments, the ebony parts are replaced with other inexpensive hard wood that is stained or painted black.

The Wood Grain - There is some difference of opinion with respect to the importance of the grain of the wood of a violin, viola, cello, or double bass. It is certainly important when evaluating the appearance of an instrument, for a beautiful piece of well-grained wood is just that, beautiful. The question of the effect of the grain on sound production arises when one sees the instruments made by Stradivari and Amati. Although some of these highly prized instruments were fabricated of beautifully grained woods, others were not. And yet, these less attractive instruments are as highly rated as their more attractive siblings. One must conclude that it is the inherent structure of the wood, rather than its grain alone, combined with the workmanship of the luthier that are the significant factors for an instrument's ultimate sound production.

Purfling - Purfling is the inlay of wood that surrounds the edge of the body of a string instrument. Chapter 4 explains how these two thin strips of hard wood are usually of a contrasting type to the wood used for the body. The purfling is recessed into the edge of the top and back plates to the depth of about a sixteenth of an inch on a violin and proportionately deeper for the larger instruments.

The exact depth is determined by the luthier. The function of purfling is to reinforce the edges of the instrument to prevent chipping and cracking. Purfling is also used by more sophisticated luthiers to control the vibration of the wood and in so doing modify the sound production.

A close examination of the degree of perfection with which the purfling has been installed can also be a measure of the luthier's skills. The
most difficult part of the purfling to install is the point at the tip of each
bout where the two strips meet. The degree of perfection with which this
is achieved is an indicator of the luthier's skill. Instruments of a lesser
quality will have a parallel line painted in place of a real inlay.

The scroll of an instrument is also an indication of the maker's skills
or lack thereof. On the better instruments, one can easily see the finesse of
craftsmanship and the luthier's personal adaptation of the basic scroll
shape. Although at first glance by the nonprofessional, all scrolls look
about the same. Placing several instruments side by side will quickly
show how they differ. The quality and individuality of a scroll is interest-
ing to observe and can add to or detract from the esthetic appeal of the
instrument; however, it should not be a significant factor in deciding on
one's final selection.

The Finish - String instrument bodies are finished with spirit or oil based
varnish to protect the wood. History abounds with speculation concerning the importance of the varnish from the past and its effect on the
sound of the instruments. Suffice to say that at this writing, no conclusion
has been reached on the validity of those theories. It is important to note
that the substance used to finish an instrument can affect the sound if that
product tends to dry to a ridged state or if it is has been given too thick a
coat. The optimum application should be of sufficient clarity and flexibility as to not impede the vibration of the wood.

4. Play the Instrument

The next step and the most important one in selecting an instrument
from the violin family is to hear the instrument under consideration and
to feel how it responds to the player. This phase of the evaluation process
is the most subjective, for all of the instrument's responses will be judged
on the basis of a player's previous musical experiences, musical taste,
ability to perform, and ability to discern minute yet significant differences
in the composition of the sounds being produced.

Violin family instruments are as unique as human beings and so
when one unique individual begins to search for the one unique instrument that will satisfy his or her needs and expectations, the search itself
becomes unique. One can like filet of sole and another filet mignon. Both
are filets, both are food, and both satisfy hunger and provide protein-rich
nourishment. Which is better? Neither. They are entirely different foods

to satisfy entirely different individual tastes. Such is the case with string instruments. The choice is individual and totally subjective. Entirely different products can be successful candidates for different individuals.

The Process - Judging an instrument for its productivity is a very complex process. Sound, and an instrument's potential to provide it are made up of many diverse components. The most important is the synergy among the instrument's capacity to respond, the bow being used, and the player's ability to maximize that potential.

Amplitude - The first step in evaluating an instrument's sound should consist of listening for amplitude or the volume of sound the instrument can produce. The instrument should project the sound in a manner that sustains or resonates sufficiently to carry on to the next note but not so much as to confuse subsequent sounds. Start by bowing each individual open string. Use a strong, separate, down bow stroke releasing the bow from the string immediately to allow it to resound. Listen to the resonance of the sound and measure its duration after the bow leaves the string. Better instruments will resound longer; lesser instruments, shorter. Proceed to use the same process with a progression of fingered notes on each string to hear how the instrument responds to that action. Now go through the same process using pizzicato, and allowing it to resonate. A responsive instrument should continue to resound after each note is plucked.

Tone Quality - The question of sound quality, also a very subjective issue, should be taken into consideration. General terms used to identify sounds are bright, dark, mellow, harsh, aggressive, warm, full-bodied, and others. To make a sound judgment, no pun intended, one must first test the four open strings. Play them with long, legato bowing with a volume ranging from ppp to fff. Close your eyes and concentrate on the quality of the sound you are hearing. Try to describe it using any of the adjectives mentioned above or any others that may come to mind as you listen. If you hear an instrument that pleases you, bingo, that's for you. Keep that instrument on the "A" list and continue as follows.

Balance - The next important element one must consider is the consistency with which the instrument produces that sound quality on the four different strings and in the seven possible positions that can be played on the instrument. Compare the sound produced on each string with that produced on the other strings. Balance, that is, equal ability to produce sound across the strings, is a measure of a good instrument. Ideally, it should perform with consistent splendor at every point on the instrument. Such a result is not very likely but the closer one comes to perfection the better.

Procedure - The most effective way to hear the true sound of an instrument is to play a simple major scale slowly with full bow starting from the lowest open string in first position and proceeding up into all seven positions. It is most unlikely that one will find all pitches producing equally, but, again, the closer the balance of sound of the notes to each other, the better. If the player is satisfied with the instrument thus far, it is then time to play it in every way possible, using exercises and music of every kind. If the instrument feels comfortable and produces to the expectations of the player, things are going well.

Since a string instrument sounds different to the player than to a listener, the last best test would be to have someone other than the principal player play the instrument. The person doing the selecting should try to listen to the instrument from every possible distance and vantage point. If satisfied, buy it.

How Do I Buy One?

In a word, carefully. Violins, violas, cellos, and double basses that are manufactured and marketed by brand name most often have a manufacturer's recommended retail price and sport a price tag. If you have selected such an instrument, you have a point of reference from which you can proceed to bargain. In the major metropolitan areas, it is not uncommon to get a discount of between 30 and 40% off that manufacturer's recommended retail price. Those discounts are entirely up to the dealer and the immediate market in which the instrument is being sold.

Handmade - If an instrument is handmade and the luthier is selling it, he is free to ask any price he feels he can get. The buyer on the other hand is free to bargain toward the goal of paying as little as possible. Let the games begin.

Used - Used instruments present a different problem in that they can be more difficult to identify in terms of value and origin. If an instrument is 50 years old and has a label with the name Stradivari or any other famous name from the past in it, don't get excited. That label is only telling you that the instrument is a copy of the shape that was used by that maker from the past.

It is a generally accepted opinion that older instruments will sound better than new ones of equal value. A new one will improve with age whereas an old one has already done so. If you select an older instrument that is in excellent condition, the sound you hear will remain as it is. If the instrument is new and of reasonable quality, the sound will more likely improve with age.

Pricing - The pricing of older instruments is open to the market. Of value is one that is in excellent condition, made with beautifully grained high quality woods, has an excellent finish, and most importantly produces the sound the buyer is seeking. Sound and condition are of greatest importance. Appearance is secondary but a good looking instrument is always better than one that is not. The absence of visual beauty should not necessarily be a deterrent. If the instrument is structurally solid and produces an excellent sound, it is certainly worth serious consideration. The converse is not so. A beautiful instrument that does not meet the sound tests should not be considered unless its intended use is as a wall hanging.

Size - Selecting the correct size for a player is of paramount importance. In order to assume a correct playing position, play in tune, produce the best possible tone and be comfortable doing so, one must have an instrument with proportions that will fit the player's anatomical individuality. Size does matter and so one must be sure that the size instrument purchased is appropriate for the player. This of course raises the question of whether it is prudent to buy an instrument other than one suited for a fully grown player. If one were to buy a 1/32 size violin for a very young player and that student continues to play the violin until adulthood, it will be necessary to buy eight violins to arrive at full size. For the solution to that problem, see chapter 6 on how to rent an instrument. For a complete listing of violin, viola, cello, and double bass sizes, see chapter 3.

Advice - Before buying a string instrument, consult a teacher to determine the size and quality instrument that would best serve the student. In most cases, a wise teacher will recommend a rental program instead of the purchase of a smaller than full (4/4) size, or in the case of the double bass, three quarter size instrument. Most rental programs will provide size changes as needed at any time without charge. Once again, buying will require the purchase of as many instruments as exist from the size the student begins on to a full size.

How to Choose and Buy a Bow

Selecting and buying a bow can be as difficult as doing so for an instrument but with a different set of challenges. The good news is a bow has fewer parts to evaluate. The process is simpler for a beginner's bow than for an upgrade model.

In chapter 4 the phrase "good instrument + bad bow = bad sound" summarized the issue in the simplest terms. A bow should be matched to the instrument for which it will be used. Like any item, bows are available at every quality level from junk to magnificent. The first step in making a choice is to learn and understand how a bow is made (see chapter 4) and then to understand what qualities one should seek in a bow that will serve the player and the instrument with which that bow will be used. The factors to be evaluated are the material from which the stick is made, the kind of hair it has, the balance of the bow, its camber, the stability of the frog, its ease of movement, and, finally, and cosmetic adornments if present, if needed, and if desired.

The Stick - The stick of a bow is its spine. It can be made of any wood or some manmade substances such as carbon fiber or fiberglass. For wooden bows, the preference is Pernambuco, an increasingly rare and expensive choice. A second choice would be a high grade of Brazil wood. The term Brazil wood is used rather loosely and can mean any kind of wood grown in Brazil. The country of origin is not a guarantee of quality because, obviously, any kind of wood can come from Brazil. It is essential that a wood other than Pernambuco be of a high quality.

Carbon fiber bows have advanced in quality and design to the point where they are considered by many to be perfectly acceptable replacements for wood. Carbon fiber bows are available in many price levels, some ranging to $500 and more. If being considered, these bows should be put through the same tests as those for a wooden bow.

Fiberglass bow sticks with horsehair are comparatively low priced, durable, do not warp, and are widely used for beginning students. These bows are excellent substitutes for wood.

When inspecting a wooden bow stick, look for a consistently dense grain with no imperfections, knots, or blemishes throughout the stick. It should be strong yet flexible and resilient enough to bend easily, but not so much as to contact the hair while playing or bend to either side to any great degree.

Camber is the curve in a bow stick. Check the degree of curve with the bow hair loose. Then tighten the hair until it is about one quarter of an inch from the center of the stick at the midpoint of the bow. This will approximate playing tension. Examine the camber to assure that it has maintained its arc while under that tension. With that same tension, look down the stick from the frog end to determine if the bow is straight. There should be no deviation from true.

The flexibility of bow sticks can vary greatly from one bow to another. Here, a matter of personal choice is the primary deciding factor. Softer sticks tend to be more yielding to pressure and, consequently, result in a generally gentler response. A stiffer stick will respond with a crisper, more aggressive sound.

Stick Shape - Bow sticks are made either octagonal or round. Round sticks are octagonal at the frog but then become round shortly after the frog. Octagonal sticks tend to be firmer than round sticks. As stated above, stiffer bows are generally a bit more responsive than round, more flexible sticks which tend to produce a gentler response. The choice is up to the player; however, unless a particularly strong opinion in one direction or the other is the player's intention for that particular bow, it is best to strike a midpoint in the choice.

The Frog - The frog is the only part of the bow that moves. Check the fit of the frog by holding the stick with one hand and with the other hand try to move the frog from side to side. It should not move. When turning the screw at the end of the bow, the frog should slide back and forth easily while remaining firmly on the stick. On the back of a frog there may be a strip of metal leading up to the bow stick. This strip is called a lining. If it is present, the frog is called fully lined; if not present it is called half lined. The difference is of little relevance and should not be a major consideration in bow selection.

Balance - Bow balance and weight rank high in the "consistency of inconsistency" category of opinions and arguments in the music world. The weight of a bow, usually measured in grams, can vary as much as fifteen grams within the same instrument category. The average weight of a violin bow is around 60 grams with the viola, cello, and double bass increasing from that 60 gram weight in 10 gram increments.

There is no correct numerical weight for a particular bow. The correct weight is that which is comfortable and responsive for the individual using it. The same is the case for balance. Hold the bow under consideration horizontal to the floor with proper hand position and with no instrument. Bounce the bow in mid-air and then move it in every direction, duplicating all possible playing motions. Repeat that action with several other bows in order to establish a baseline for the feel. There will be distinct differences in the feel of each bow. Then play the same brief passage with each of those same bows. One will be outstanding. Buy it.

Summary - A bow is as important a part of an instrument outfit as is the instrument itself. Bow selection, often given short shrift, should take place after the instrument is selected and with that instrument at the trial. Decide on a price range, the level of the player, the quality of the instrument for which the bow is intended, and the type of stick desired. With that information at hand, proceed as advised above. For beginners, a fiberglass bow with horsehair is usually the first choice by most teachers because of its strength, durability, consistent weight, camber, and balance. If that is the choice there is little need to go through the testing process because with very few exceptions, fiberglass bows made by the same manufacturer are reliably the same.

When selecting other bows, the trial procedure is essential with the bottom line being how it sounds to the ear of the player and how it feels as it is being used to make those sounds. Having the opinion of a listener who is not playing will also aid in the decision making process, but it is the player who should make the final decision. Softer, more flexible sticks will make smoother, warmer sounds while stronger, less flexible sticks will produce a brighter, more aggressive sound. The choice is personal.

Chapter 6
How to Rent an Instrument

Renting a musical instrument is a multi-step process requiring an understanding of the many pitfalls in the market, a basic knowledge of the instrument being sought, and due diligence on the part of the renter. Following the steps outlined in this chapter will lead to a successful rental experience at a reasonable cost.

Musical instrument rental programs abound throughout the United States. They can be found anywhere from the local mom and pop music shops to national franchises on the Internet. The reason for this abundance? It is a good business. Unfortunately, because of the almost universal lack of consumer knowledge, it is a better business for the rental shop than for the consumers. These are usually parents of early grade school children who, for whatever reason, have decided to study an instrument. A laudable venture, the study of music has been proven to significantly advance learning skills in many areas. Unfortunately, most students never really achieve a high level of proficiency on their instruments but they do enjoy playing for a few years in various school bands and orchestras and the overall experience is highly beneficial.

Most students do not become proficient because they don't practice. This is a great advantage to the rental company for the less the student practices, the less the wear and tear on the instrument. Sad but true. The rental companies' best customer is the one who is a long time mediocre member of a school band or orchestra.

Musical instruments are very complex and, as a result, few people know much about them. A nonprofessional out to acquire an instrument by either rental or purchase is a babe in the woods. The best protection is to consult with the music teacher on what to rent, what to look for when renting, and where to rent it. Be sure to rent it with an option to return, exchange, or replace it within a prescribed period of time. Then ask the teacher to check the instrument within that time period so the dealer can make any adjustments to the instrument if needed.

When renting an instrument, the first concern should be with its cleanliness. No professional knowledge is needed for one to see that the instrument, bow, and case are clean and that those items have no major visible defects. A good quality professional rental service will present an instrument that is either new, is not new but looks new, or is at least in good playing condition, clean and properly prepared. (See chapter 5 to review the process of checking an instrument of the violin family.) The instrument should be free from rosin dust especially under the bridge, and on the strings in the bowing area between the bridge and fingerboard. Bow hair should be clean and properly rosined, showing no dark area near the frog. If the renter has had previous music instruction, the next best step is to try the instrument by playing a few simple scales on all strings.

Rental plans can range from a handshake to a multi-page, fine print contract tying the renter into a plan that will ultimately cost more than the instrument is worth. Caveat emptor! This phase of the rental process requires no knowledge about instruments. It requires the renter to apply due diligence by acquiring information on all the rental plans available. One must read and understand the contracts for each plan and carefully calculate the costs, not based on the initial charge, for that is often a loss leader, but on the ongoing cost as the player continues with the rental plan. A competent teacher will have done all this in advance of recommending a particular company; however, it is always best to double check to be sure that one is getting the best deal. "A great music teacher does not always a good business person make."

Musical instrument rental plans can range in time and cost from a simple school year rental for a one-time fee to every arrangement conceivable by man. The following are some of the plans available:

Month-to-Month Rental

This is not recommended because, although it may appeal to the parent to be able to opt out at any time with as little investment as possible, it also permits the student to opt out of study if s/he has a particularly tough week. Studies show that committing to the rental of an instrument for a year has the effect of committing to study for a year.

Three Month Starter with Renewal

This is a particularly dangerous one for it introduces the rental as a loss leader with an introductory period for a small price and then follows that with ballooning costs not easily found in the small print of the contract. If the renter does the math, the ultimate cost over an average student rental period can end up being much more than the value of the instrument.

One Semester at a Time Rental

If the price is right, this may be O.K. except for the fact that, as in the month-to-month rental, the option to quit mid-year is open and the mid-year renewal will make the total year cost higher. This is not the best choice.

School Year Rental

This is the most common and usually the most equitable plan because (A) the time period coincides with the school program, (B) the student is committed to the program for the school year, (C) the price is usually the best of all the rental time periods and, (D) a reliable company will usually give the summer to follow with no charge if the next school year's payment is made prior to the summer recess. When one uses this plan, be sure it includes a provision for instrument exchanges at any time with no charge for the same priced instrument or a prorated price for a more expensive one.

Full Year (12 month) Rental

This program is best used if the student wants to begin study in at the end of the school year with the intention of continuing to study in the following school year. Again, when using this plan, be sure it includes a provision for instrument exchanges at any time with no additional charge for the same priced or lesser priced instrument or a prorated price for a more expensive one.

Rent-to-Own

This program is appealing at first glance until one gets into the weeds of the contract. The question here is do you want to own the first instrument you get? Students, especially young ones, because of their lack of experience in handling an instrument usually cause more wear and tear than they will as they progress. Also, there is often some likelihood that the student may want to change instruments, so the possibility of a change should be included in the contract. As a student progresses, s/he may need a better quality instrument. Does the contract allow for upgrades? If so, at what cost?

The major issue in the rent-to-own program is the true value of the instrument and its ultimate cost to the consumer over the rental period. These programs often lack specificity in stating the true value of the instrument in question. The advertising will focus on the low monthly payments with little or no reference to the total cost at the end of the contract. Most important is the total price being charged for the instrument.

In many cases, it is full list price. Keep in mind the fact that it is easy to obtain a least a 30-40% discount on the purchase of any instrument on line or even in a local music store. In some cases that discounted price can be paid over time or at least put on a credit card that the consumer can pay over a convenient period of time.

Renting an Upgrade Instrument

The rental of a better than beginner quality instrument is often sought by advancing students. A rental program should allow for this change at any time with a differential cost to the consumer. One should seek guidance from a professional on the brand and model instrument to rent. It is unreasonable to expect a rental service to provide upgrade instruments at the same price as beginner instruments; however, the higher price should be proportionate to the higher value of the upgrade. In the case of string instruments where brand names are not necessarily a consistent indicator of a particular quality, one should seek the advice of a teacher or other professional in the decision making process.

In summary, one must evaluate the quality of the instrument being provided and the entire final cost to the consumer. Will it reflect some kind of reasonable discount or will it end up being full list price or greater? Consider the fact that the dealer will have to wait a period of time for full payment and so is entitled to a reasonable margin of profit, but there should also be some form of discount built into the program that will benefit the consumer.

Renting a New Instrument

Some parents and students prefer to rent a new instrument. Expect to do this at a higher cost than the traditional used instrument program. The cost and the rental program will vary depending on the dealer, the quality of the instrument, and its retail value. Renting a new instrument for a beginning student should only be necessary if there are no used instruments available. A reliable company with professional standards can easily provide a used instrument for a lesser price. In the case of the instruments in the violin family, there is little advantage to renting a new instrument because generally, new string instruments produce harsher sounds than older ones.

Renting an Old Instrument

Old non-fretted string instruments of good quality are sometime offered for rental by either an individual shop owner or by the more sophisticated larger companies. An old violin of good quality can be a very good aid to learning for an advanced, mature student who is able to maximize the instrument's potential while caring for it properly. The consumer must check the instrument carefully to ascertain the instrument's structural viability and stability.

When the instrument passes a physical inspection, it is then necessary to determine if it is capable of producing the sound desired by the student. For this process, see part 1 of chapter 5, item number 4 above. One must play the instrument and put it through the paces as described in that section. If the player is satisfied with the physical structure and the sound it produces, rent it. Regarding the cost of renting such an instrument, the market is wide open for a determination of price by the consumer and the merchant.

Renting a Shopworn Instrument

The term shopworn is used to describe an instrument that shows some evidence of wear. It can take the form of scratches, chips, wear on the edges of the top and back, or any other kind of blemish. Assuming the instrument performs as it should, these defects are cosmetic and should have no effect on the instrument's productivity. Some companies specialize in such rentals, offering them at significantly lower prices than the more attractive instruments. Providing the student does not object, such a rental is usually a good deal monetarily.

Additional Charges

Along with the rental plans there can be add-ons such as damage protection, loss protection, and a long list of accessories and learning aids.

Damage Protection

Damage protection is insurance which covers any damage that may occur under *normal use*. The operative words here are normal use. Vandalism or deliberate destruction is usually omitted from this coverage so if the child is inclined to vent his/her frustrations on the instrument, the parent should be prepared to pay for the damage.

The cost of this insurance can vary greatly. It is predicated on the value of the instrument along with whatever the market will bear. The prices can range from $20.00 for a school year to as much as $20.00 per month. This is one of several places where an unscrupulous merchant can take advantage of a consumer, so remember to include this cost in your calculation of total rental cost for the year. It is possible that a higher extra fee may give you pause to seek another dealer.

Loss Protection

This is insurance against loss but again there are caveats to this kind of coverage. One can't just claim an instrument as being lost and expect to get it replaced. Usually the coverage is effective only in certain locations such as the school, at home or from a car, or under certain conditions such as fire or burglary. A police report and a statement from the principal of the school from which the instrument is stolen, along with other documentation, are usually required to process a claim.

The cost of this insurance can also vary greatly. It too is predicated on the value of the instrument along with whatever the market will bear. Like the damage protection, the prices can range from $20.00 for a school year to as much as $20.00 per month. Again, this is also one of several places where an unscrupulous merchant can take advantage of a consumer, so remember to include this cost in your calculation of the total rental cost for the year. It is possible that the loss of a rented instrument is covered under one's homeowner's or valuable items policy so check with your insurance broker before signing up for this coverage with the music dealer. If this extra cost is excessive, you may want to consider seeking another dealer.

One additional consideration that is of some importance is the procedure for servicing a rental instrument that is offered by the rental company. A full service company will offer an in-school pick-up and delivery service where permitted. With this program, the consumer will call the company for the service. They will assign a pick-up day and specific location to leave the instrument in the school in which the instruction is being provided. The instrument will be picked up and returned to that location within a reasonable time or sometimes replaced with another instrument. If the rental company is local, there may be a location where the renter can bring the instrument in for prompter service.

Summary

Much thought and research should precede the rental of an instrument if the renter expects to end up on the winning end of this procedure. Renter, beware! What can appear to be a few dollars a month expense can, over time, and the study of a musical instrument is over time, end up costing hundreds if not thousands of dollars more than would be necessary if the consumer was prudent in the initial steps.

Chapter 7
How to Take Care of Your Instrument

Unlike many of the items one uses in daily life, a musical instrument requires a very specific regimen of care if it is to function properly and have a long life. This chapter will outline the process.

All instruments of the violin family must be thought of as being structurally dynamic because they are made almost entirely of wood held together with temperature sensitive, water-based hide glue. Because wood is hygroscopic, its cellular structure provides a natural repository for moisture, making these instruments an excellent reactor to both the negative and positive effects of moisture. As a result, the instrument physically responds to the environment in which it lives.

Since string instruments have the capacity to absorb or release moisture, it is essential for their well-being that they live in a climate which is well balanced in both temperature and humidity. If the climate is too dry, there is a danger of cracking. Conversely, too moist a climate can result in seams and glued joints opening, wood warping, and for the formation of mold.

Should a crack occur or seam open, it is important to avoid touching that area. Any deposit of skin oils or perspiration can inhibit the effectiveness of the glue used in the repair process. If a crack occurs in a place where there is a possibility of structural damage to the instrument, those places being at the sound post, bass bar or neck/fingerboard joints, the strings should be loosened and bridge taken down immediately to avoid any further damage. Before removing the bridge, place a soft cloth under the tailpiece to avoid scratching the body.

Another possible reaction to extremes in climate can be the raising or lowering of the top of an instrument with the bridge and strings responding likewise. This is especially common in cellos and in the double bass. More on this to follow. Moisture during a summer season can raise the top, and drying out caused by winter central heating can lower the top. In such cases, the owner of an instrument which responds in this manner can have several bridges of different heights on hand to accommodate those changes. An alternative to the several bridges is an adjustable bridge which can be raised or lowered by turning a screw installed on each leg. See chapter 8 on Accessories for more on the adjustable bridge.

In summary, an owner of a violin, viola, cello, or double bass must be cognizant of the fact that the various woods from which these instruments are made respond to changes in temperature and humidity by expanding and contracting with different degrees of intensity. This dynamic can often result in open seams, cracking which can occur anywhere, warping of the neck and fingerboard, slipping pegs and various small parts becoming loose as the glue dries out. Should any of these occur, there is no need for alarm because, if properly dealt with, none of these events will significantly affect the performance or value of the instrument. They are just part of the process of living with an instrument made of wood. The possibility of this happening should be given consideration when planning a maintenance schedule.

The Process

String instrument maintenance falls into several categories. These are storage, cleaning, and minor adjustments. Major repairs should be left to the professionals.

Storage

When not in use, a string instrument should always be kept in a case, stored in an environment that is comfortable for a human being, i.e., not too hot, too cold, too dry, or too humid. Extreme temperature and humidity can cause damage as described above.

When traveling with an instrument, the same rules apply. Keep the instrument in the same location you occupy when traveling. The trunk of a car or luggage compartment of a bus or plane are not acceptable places for storage in travel. Keep the instrument as close as possible to the temperature in which you reside.

Cleaning

After each use, wipe the surfaces of the instrument and the strings with a soft cotton cloth to remove any rosin dust, natural skin oils, and perspiration. These will accumulate and, if left to permeate the surface of the instrument, will cause damage that could affect the sound and diminish the instrument's value.

A good instrument is finished with either spirit or oil based varnish. This finish is similar to that of a piece of fine furniture but much more delicate. Because of its sound producing function, any violin family instrument is more sensitive to any treatment that may affect the molecular structure of the wood. Therein lies the rub (my second unintentional pun). The decision on what to use is open to opinion and should be considered based on the individual instrument, its owner's feelings on the matter, and perhaps consultation with a teacher or professional luthier. At the discretion of the owner, periodic use of a cleaning agent should be scheduled as needed. There is some difference of opinion on the use of polishes of any kind. One will find numerous polishes on the market, each touting its own benefits, be they real or contrived. Inexpensive instruments are subject to the same hazards as better instruments with one exception. Often they are finished with a coat of sprayed-on lacquer. In this case, any good quality furniture polish can be used without serious consequences.

Minor Adjustments

Non-fretted instruments need constant minor adjustments. The primary adjustment, which is ongoing, is that of tuning.

The Tuning Process

The violin, viola, and cello all have wedge shaped wooden pegs which are forced into holes in the peg box. These instruments use the same tuning procedure.

1. For the violin and viola, hold the instrument on your lap with the scroll up and the strings facing you. For the cello, hold the instrument on its endpin on the floor with the strings facing you.

2. Using a piano, pitch pipe, or electric tuner, select and produce the correct pitch for the string you are tuning.

3. When you have the pitch firmly fixed in your mind, pluck the string to be tuned. The next step is vital to successful tuning.

4. While the string is sounding the note you have just plucked, slowly tighten the string by turning the peg up or down as needed, and, as you turn the peg, push in so that it is forced into the holes of the peg box (Fig. 7.1).

N.B. If you do not force the peg into the peg holes, the peg will not hold the string in tune.

Figure 7.1 Tuning

5. While you are slowly turning and pushing the peg in, listen to the sound of the string changing in pitch. When it reaches the pitch you have in mind, stop. The string will be tuned.

6. If necessary, you can further adjust the pitch in small degrees by tightening or loosening the fine tuner (Fig. 7.2).

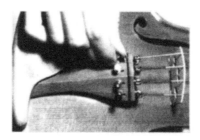

Figure 7.2 Fine Tuning

7. For a more advanced player, bowing the string being tuned while adjusting the peg or fine tuner will allow for a greater degree of pitch accuracy. A still more advanced player may want to bow double stops, two strings simultaneously to create perfect fifths. A trained ear will find using that interval most effective in the tuning process.

Tuning the Double Bass

Because of the greater thickness of the strings, the double bass uses a worm and gear system to tune and maintain accurate intonation (Fig. 7.3).

This system merely requires turning the peg in the direction needed with no pushing action.

Figure 7.3 Worm and Gear System

1. Hold the bass in playing position.

2. Using a piano, pitch pipe, or an electric tuner, select and produce the correct pitch for the string you are tuning.

3. When you have the pitch firmly fixed in your mind, bow the string to be tuned. Because strings on the double bass are lower pitched, bowing rather than plucking will produce a sound more easily heard for tuning purposes.

4. While the string is sounding the note you are bowing, turn the machine gear peg up or down as needed.

5. When the sound reaches the pitch you have in mind, the string will be tuned. Experienced players can further fine tune their instrument through the use of harmonics. By bowing the string being tuned and touching it at a spot about mid-way on the string, one can break the vibrating pattern and produce a falsetto-like note which is easier to hear and permits a more refined pitch adjustment. The operative word in this paragraph is "experienced." It takes a bit of practice to perform this procedure effectively; however, it is most effective on the lower pitched instruments as it produces a higher pitch easier to hear for tuning purposes.

If the process described above is followed carefully and the wooden pegs do not hold, then there could be a problem with their fit. Improperly installed or worn pegs or peg holes will not hold securely. If the problem is not too severe, minor adjustments can be made with the use of commercially sold peg treatments, which can take the form of drops or pastes (see chapter 8). Seek the advice of a professional regarding which product is best for this condition.

Adjusting the Bridge

The Violin and Viola - As strings are tuned, they gradually pull the bridge toward the fingerboard in small, almost unnoticeable increments. To prevent the bridge from falling or warping, it will be necessary to adjust it slightly back toward the tailpiece as needed. This adjustment is achieved for the violin or viola by first loosening the strings and then placing the instrument on one's lap with the fingerboard facing away from one's body. Using the thumb and forefinger of each hand, grip the bridge on either side and bend it back to its upright position. The bridge feet should be in perfect contact with the top of the instrument. Re-tune the instrument.

The Cello - For the cello, loosen the strings slightly. Then hold the cello in playing position, lean over the shoulders of the instrument to reach down to the bridge, and with the thumb and forefinger of each hand, grip the bridge on either side and bend it back to its upright position. Re-tune the cello.

The Double Bass - For the double bass, loosen the strings slightly, lay the instrument on its back on a soft rug surface and move the bridge to its upright position. Then re-tune the bass.

For All Instruments - After tuning, make a quick check of the bridge viewing it from the tailpiece side to be sure that the feet are in total contact with the top of the instrument. When viewing the bridge from its side, the side facing the tailpiece should be at a perfect 90 degree angle from the top of the instrument whereas the fingerboard side of the bridge will be graduated to a smaller thickness toward its top.

Placement - The next observation to make is the placement of the bridge on the top of the instrument. There are two directions to check. Note the small notch that is cut into the center area of each side of the "f" hole. Those notches are an indicator of the optimum bridge position between the fingerboard and tailpiece for that particular instrument. There can be some latitude in that placement if an experienced luthier determines an-

bass bar while the right foot stands slightly behind (toward the fingerboard side) the sound post. In this position the right foot of the bridge conducts the higher tones to the top of the instrument and down to the sound post, which then carries the sound to the back of the instrument. The left foot conducts the lower tones to the bass bar which transverses lengthwise along the instrument and distributes the sound across the top (Fig. 7.4).

Figure 7.4 Bridge

Bridge Dimensions — Since the bridge plays a dominant role in transferring the sound from the string to the body of the instrument, the design and material used to make the bridge, how it is cut to fit the instrument, and its placement on the instrument must be calculated to fill its function in the best possible way.

The dimensions for string instrument bridges are unique to each instrument. Although there are some guidelines for the initial cutting of the bridge (Fig. 7.5), the final product must be cut to fit the contour of the top of each individual instrument and to provide sufficient, but not excessive height for the strings to clear the fingerboard.

The height of a bridge determines the distance it will elevate the strings above the end of the fingerboard at two points — the highest and lowest pitched strings. The two intermediate strings are set proportionately, following the contour of the end of the fingerboard. If the strings are proportionately set, the player will be able to bow each string comfortably without inadvertently bowing two strings simultaneously. Serious consideration must also be given to the spacing of the strings across the top of the bridge so they will span evenly over the fingerboard, starting from the nut and extending over the bridge to the tailpiece.

fortably without inadvertently bowing two strings simultaneously. Serious consideration must also be given to the spacing of the strings across the top of the bridge so they will span evenly over the fingerboard, starting from the nut and extending over the bridge to the tailpiece.

	STRING HEIGHT FROM FINGERBOARD	BRIDGE THICKNESS	STRING SPACING
VIOLIN	E 1/8" G 3/16"	1/16"	7/16"
VIOLA	A 3/16" C 1/4"	1/16"	1/2"
CELLO	A 1/4" C 5/16"	3/32"	5/8"
BASS	G 7/16" E 11/16"	3/16"	1-1/8"

Figure 7.5 Bridge Height Chart

Bridge Inserts - The most common material used for bridges is hard maple. It is essential that the wood be hard, because it must withstand the pressure and friction of the taut strings. Sometimes inserts of even harder material are used (especially at the point on the bridge where the violin "E" string makes contact) in order to withstand the cutting action of that very thin, taut string. Ebony, cowhide, rubber, or plastic is used in various ways to help prevent wear on the point of contact where the strings meet the bridge.

Climate Change - An issue with bridge height sometimes occurs when the belly or top of an instrument rises or lowers with a change in the temperature and humidity. This occurs less often in the violin and viola, but more frequently in the cello and double bass. When the climate changes from cold and dry to warm and humid, the wood of string instruments reacts by expanding in a hot humid environment and contracting in a dry colder environment. Moisture during a summer season can raise the top, and drying out caused by winter central heating can lower the top. As this expansion and contraction occurs and the top of the larger instruments rises or falls, the height of the bridge in relation to the fingerboard changes. In such cases, the owner of an instrument which responds in this manner can have several bridges of different heights on hand to accommodate for those changes. An alternative to the several bridges is an adjustable bridge which can be raised or lowered by turning a screw installed on each leg. See Figure 8.36 in chapter 8 on Accessories for more on the adjustable bridge.

Maintaining the Pegs

Sticking and Slipping - An ongoing problem with violins, violas, and cellos is slipping or sticking pegs. As the seasons change, the wooden pegs which are usually made of ebony or boxwood but can be of other hard woods, expand with the increase in humidity and temperature or contract with cold dry air. The peg box in which the pegs are installed is usually made of hard maple. This wood follows the same seasonal pattern of expansion and contraction; however, it does so at a different rate from that of the pegs. The result is slipping or sticking pegs. The double bass does not have this problem because of the worm-in-gear mechanism used on those instruments.

Over the past three hundred plus years, the treatment for these problems has taken various forms. Some find applying chalk or soap to the pegs will alleviate the sticking problem. One will find a variety of peg treatments on the market, all claiming to solve the problem. Many of the most popular products are listed in chapter 8 on accessories.

A common cause of slipping pegs is improper wrapping of the string around the peg. In this case, wound string buildup at either end of the peg can prevent it from being fully seated in the peg hole. The hole that is drilled in the peg to receive a string should be at the narrow end of the peg. Starting from that point where the string is inserted into the hole, the string should be wound concentrically with the windings aligned firmly against each other as they progress toward the ear end of the peg. If the string is installed in this manner, there is no string buildup and the peg will move easily. A wound string on a peg must not be allowed to build up against the peg box since this can cause damage to the peg box and prevent the peg from turning freely.

Fine Tuner - A string can end in a loop, a ball, or a knot. This end of the string is attached to the tailpiece by being placed directly into the keyhole-shaped hole, or it can be connected to a fine tuner, a metal device that is attached to a tailpiece to receive the string. The fine tuner mechanism enables the player to achieve perfect tuning up or down in minute degrees by turning a screw.

Chapter 8 will tell more about the different kinds of fine tuners available. Figure 7.6 shows the three different kinds of string ends, a fine tuner, and a tailpiece with a loop end string and three ball end strings attached to four fine tuners.

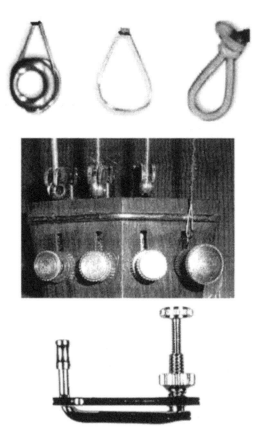

Figure 7.6 String Ends (top illustration) and Fine Tuners

A fine tuner requires periodic adjustments. When used over a period of time, the screw will be turned down more than up and will ultimately reach its lowest position rendering it useless. At that point there is also a danger of the under part of the fine tuner coming in contact with the top of the instrument (Fig 7.7). This can severely damage the varnish.

Figure 7.7 Violin Fine Tuner

It will be necessary for the player to regularly check the fine tuners and return them to their highest position before resuming normal use. Should the screws on the fine tuners become difficult to turn, a bit of graphite or any simple lubricant will resolve the problem. Use great caution to avoid having any lubricant reach the instrument's finish.

The Tailpiece - A tailpiece is held on with a tail gut that gets its name from the fact that it was originally made of gut. They are now made of nylon and have adjustment screws on both ends. The tailpiece should be attached to the end button of the instrument with the tail gut adjusted to the point where the tailpiece touches the edge of the saddle (Fig. 7.8). The tailpiece should not extend beyond the saddle.

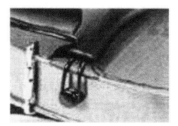

Figure 7.8 Tailpiece with Gut

Bow Sticks – A Review

The Stick - Violin bow sticks can be made of various kinds of wood. The two most popular are Pernambuco and Brazil wood. Other materials used are fiberglass, carbon fiber in various forms, and aluminum.

Pernambuco is considered to be the best wood for use because of its strength, light weight, and when properly cared for, its ability to keep its shape.

Brazil Wood is a less expensive alternative and, consequently, as such, has the same positive attributes but to a lesser degree.

Carbon Fiber bows are becoming quite popular, share the positive qualities of the wood bows, are more durable but can be as expensive as a wood bow.

Fiberglass - Fiberglass bows came into existence in the middle of the last century and have become a most popular alternative to wood for use in early study. They are inexpensive, very durable, light, well balanced, and are made with either fiberglass or real horsehair.

Aluminum - Aluminum bows were made in the mid-1950s with some success and some may still existence but they are no longer popular.

Bow Care

Wood - A wooden bow is a very delicate piece of equipment requiring consistently careful handling. Like the instruments, wood bows are also very sensitive to the atmosphere in which they live. Humidity and temperature control are necessary for a bow to live a good life. Think of the optimum environment in which you would be comfortable and that is where a bow will be safe.

Tension - The tension of the bow hair is a primary consideration. When preparing a bow for use, tighten the hair to the degree where it has enough resistance to perform as needed while the stick retains its arc in the direction of the hair. If the stick is no longer arched after the hair is tightened to playing tension, either the hair is too tight or the bow stick has lost its arc. In this case, loosen the hair to the point where it will respond as needed and, if all is well, the bow stick will resume its arc. With the same playing tension, if the bow does not show an arc, seek the advice of an expert.

Occasionally, a hair will break while in use. Do not pull it off the bow. Cut it at the frog and tip with a scissor to avoid dislodging the other hairs where they are connected at those two points. When finished using the bow, always loosen the hair to relieve the tension on the stick and on the wedges in the tip and frog that hold the hair in place.

Cleaning - Under no circumstances should the bow hair be touched with one's hand. Natural oils and perspiration will lessen the effectiveness of the bow hair. Should the bow hair become soiled or laden with rosin, the hair may be cleaned by wiping in an up and down motion with a soft cloth moistened with isopropyl alcohol. Do not let the alcohol touch the bow stick because it will damage the finish. After use, remove all rosin dust from the bow stick by wiping it with a soft cloth.

Infestation - Dermestids are a species of minute beetles found in animal material such as horsehair. These creatures are sometimes found on the hair of bows that have been improperly stored for a long period of time. Evidence of the presence of these pests would be hair falling off a bow that has not been in use. Should this situation exist, remove the bow from the case, cut off the all the hair with a scissor, discard the hair, and send the bow to a bow maker for rehairing. Next, vacuum the case thoroughly, giving special care to the corners and edges. Then spray the case with an insecticide, and let the case remain open in a bright sunlit place for a few days. If there is still evidence of infestation, replace the case. For more about bows, review chapter 2.

Horsehair

When viewed with the naked eye, horsehair appears to be smooth, but under examination with a microscope, the surface of the hair is quite rough. Particles, called follicles, project from the hair, forming an abrasive surface.

Rosin is a tree sap derivative that is applied to bow hair to increase its gripping power. Using a properly rosined bow is essential to producing a good sound. Too much rosin will cause the bow hair to grip the string too aggressively and produce a harsh sound. Too little rosin will cause the bow to slide on the string and produce a weak sound. Using the wrong rosin can result in either of these negative effects. There is no way to explain in detail how much rosin is too much or too little. This determination is solely up to the player's discretion and relies on his or her instincts to make that decision. Chapter 2 Figure 2.5 explains the interaction of the rosined bow hair with the violin string. A review will help understand the need for proper rosining of a bow. Chapter 8 will help select the correct rosin for use with each instrument.

Adjustments

Strings - Strings are in continuous contact with the nut, bridge, and tailpiece on an instrument. It is therefore important that some periodic attention be given to those points of contact to ensure that they are wearing properly and are in optimum adjustment to produce the best sound.

The Nut - The nut, which is located directly below the peg box, controls the distribution of the four strings across the fingerboard as well as the strings' distance or height from the fingerboard. As time passes, it is possible that the glue holding the nut in place will dry out and the nut can become unstable. This is an easy fix since it just has to be glued back in place.

A second and more serious problem occurs when, over time, as the strings are tuned, the slots in the nut that guide the strings will wear down. This causes the strings to be too close to the fingerboard affecting intonation and causing a buzz. If this situation occurs, it will be necessary to have a professional technician or luthier replace the nut. A small application of graphite (pencil point shavings) into each slot before the strings are installed will ease the friction of the strings on the nut, help reduce wear, and prevent the problem from happening.

The Bridge - The bridge is the next point of contact of the strings with the instrument. The previous section discusses the bridge placement in detail. As stated above in the tuning section, when strings are tuned they gradually pull the bridge toward the fingerboard in small almost unnoticeable increments. It will be necessary to periodically adjust the bridge slightly back toward the tailpiece to prevent the bridge from warping or falling down.

The Tailpiece - The next and final point of contact the strings have is with the tailpiece, which exists in a variety of forms from a simple plastic unit to the most elaborate hand carved ivory work of art. The size, density of material, and location of the tailpiece in relation to the bridge, along with the tail gut adjustment are all factors that affect the vibration of the strings. Careful attention must be given to these issues when a tailpiece is being fitted.

Tailpieces are made with one built-in fine tuner for each string or without any built-in fine tuners. Tailpieces with built-in fine tuners are made of metal or plastic and are very convenient for use with student instruments. Advanced players are usually satisfied with only one fine tuner added for the instrument's highest string. Keeping the four fine tuner tailpiece is a matter of individual choice. Tailpieces require maintenance on the adjustors and the tail gut. Both of these are discussed above in the section on tuning.

The Saddle - The saddle is a small piece of ebony or other hard wood that is placed at the end of an instrument's body. This hard wood acts as a support for the tail gut, preventing it from damaging the softer spruce wood instrument top. A saddle should be fitted so that there is sufficient space on either side for the inevitable expansion and contraction of the spruce top. If the saddle is too tightly fitted when that expansion takes place, a crack in the top at either side of the saddle could occur. Should this happen, the saddle should be refitted by a luthier and the crack repaired.

Summary

Violins, violas, cellos, and double basses require similar procedures and equipment for proper maintenance. An owner should take the time to develop an understanding of how these instruments react to their environment and to their being handled on a
long term basis. With that understanding, maintaining the instruments will be a matter of establishing simple, routine procedures to be used after each playing session along with other, more elaborate procedures to be carried out by a luthier periodically, as needed.

Chapter 8
Accessories

In order to function properly, musical instruments require the use of certain specific accessories. There are also accessories that, although not absolutely needed, can make ownership more pleasurable. This chapter shows a variety of accessories designed for use with instruments of the violin family. There are three categories of accessories available that are used to enhance the playing experience: those that are necessary, those that significantly facilitate the playing and maintenance of an instrument, and those that are luxuries. The following accessories are needed to successfully play any of the instruments in the violin family.

Rosin

Rosin is made from plant resin which is obtained from conifer (cone bearing) trees. The resin is harvested from a tree and distilled to remove the turpentine element. The remaining product is rosin. At this point in the process, a formula that is peculiar to each maker and very often kept a secret is used to produce violin, viola, cello, and double bass rosin. Some of the more common elements added to the raw rosin to improve its ability to create friction on a bow are bees' wax and metal particles. These, with the further addition of the "secret" ingredients in the formulae of the manufacturers, result in the numerous brands, types, densities, and colors of rosin available. When applied to bow hair, rosin increases the gripping action of the hair against a string. (See chapter 2, Figure 2.5.)

Rosin is made in different strengths for each of the four instruments of the violin family. Violin rosin is very different from double bass rosin, so it is essential that one use the rosin intended for the instrument being played. Rosin comes in shades of amber, graduating from light to dark. Dozens of brands are marketed with every conceivable claim to justify their unique characteristics. Prices range from 99 cents to $35. and in some "very special" cases even more. How does one choose? For a beginning student it would be prudent to start with the least expensive rosin available. It will work fine until either the teacher recommends a change or the player feels a need for something different. In most cases, the latter will never come to pass. Figure 8.1 shows a variety of different strength rosins.

Violin and Viola Rosin

Cello Rosin   Double Bass Rosin

Figure 8.1 Assorted Rosins

As is the case with many aspects of music study and performance, personal opinion is often predicated on any number of intangible subjective judgments. There is no doubt that many of the different brands of rosin have unique contents and processing procedures, but the reliability of the claims the marketers make about how those unique characteristics can improve the effectiveness of their product is somewhat dubious. Because of the numerous rosin brands and types on the market, it is necessary that this topic be discussed using general terms.

Rosin can be categorized by degree of hardness and color. Hard rosin, usually light amber in color, produces a dry powdery product when applied to bow hair. Its gripping power is lighter and more effective for use on violin strings. Soft rosin, darker in color, has a stickier texture and provides increased gripping power for the bow hair. Soft rosin is more effective for use on the bows of larger string instruments such as the cello and double bass.

The factors that affect the color of rosin are the age of the tree from which the base product is drawn and the distillation process used to convert the resin into rosin. Since rosin can be found with all degrees of hardness from very hard to very soft, it becomes the job of the player to decide on the degree of hardness that is suitable for that individual's playing needs. The desire to produce an aggressive sound might call for the use of softer rosin and the reverse applies.

Some players keep several rosins of different hardness and use them as needed for different effects. At least one rosin maker produces a cake of rosin that has hard rosin on one side and a softer product on the reverse side. This allows the player to flip the cake should s/he want to switch back and forth. The apparent drawback with this concept is that if the player uses the soft side for an aggressive sound first and then wishes to use the hard side for a less aggressive effect, there is no going back. The soft, stickier rosin will remain on the bow hair negating the powdery effect that the hard rosin would ordinarily produce. Perhaps this two-sided product is intended to permit the player to create his/her own blend by combining the two in proportions suitable to that individual's needs. Since rosin is climate sensitive and will soften with warmer temperatures and harden in colder temperatures, some players will change rosins with the seasons or with the venue in which they are performing. One can find "winter and summer" rosin on the market.

Tuning Forks

Invented in 1711 by John Shore, the tuning fork is the most basic device designed specifically for use to accurately determine pitch. The device consists of a u-shaped metal form with a handle at the base of the U (Fig. 8.2).

Figure 8.2 Tuning Fork

Holding the tuning fork by the handle, when the tines (prongs) are struck on a hard surface they are set into a vibrating pattern which produces a tone (Fig. 8.3). The tone produced is determined by the length of the tines and is pure by virtue of the fact that the dominant sound is the fundamental pitch with the few overtones present fading almost immediately.

Figure 8.3 Vibrating Tines

Pitch Pipes

Pitch pipes are a necessary accessory for any string instrument player. The simplest pitch pipe is made with four small pipes joined together (Fig. 8.4). Each pipe is tuned to match the pitch of one string on the instrument for which its use is intended. The pitches from high to low for the violin are E, A, D, and G. The viola pitches are A, D, G, and C, and the cello also A, D, G, and C but an octave lower. The double bass pitches are G, D, A, and E, the reverse order of the violin. The player gently blows into the appropriate pipe to hear the desired pitch needed to tune a string.

Figure 8.4 Simple Violin Pitch Pipe

A chromatic pitch pipe is round and contains a marked opening for every pitch in the chromatic scale (Fig. 8.5). The notes start at C and progress chromatically up an octave to the next C in the scale. The player can choose any note, slide the white marker to that note's position on the pitch pipe, blow into that hole, and hear the pitch selected.

Figure 8.5 Chromatic Pitch Pipe

Electronic Tuners

There are two kinds of electronic tuners available. The simpler type produces the four pitches of the open strings for a specific instrument. A more comprehensive model offers a complete chromatic scale from which to select a pitch. The player selects the pitch needed, presses the required button for that sound generator and hears the pitch (Fig. 8.6).

Figure 8.6 Electronic Tuner

A more advanced type of device shows an image of the pitch being produced. (Fig. 8.7). When the player bows or plucks an open string, a needle on a screen will indicate if the sound is up, down, or spot-on in relation to the actual pitch being sought. If necessary, the player can then adjust the string up or down until the correct pitch is reached.

Figure 8.7 Electronic Tuner with Screen

Apps or Applications

The speed at which technology is advancing precludes this author's going into any detail on this subject for fear that by the time this sentence is complete, the facts will once again have changed. Apps and websites on any music topic abound. Aids to tuning appear on websites, iPads, iPhones, the Internet, and whatever else will be invented by the time this book is published. If one were so inclined, there may be some advantage to taking this route for tuning assistance; however, in doing so, it would be wise to keep in mind that the objective of this exercise is to tune one's instrument. Try to avoid being distracted by the intrigue of technology and in so doing utilize practice time to get involved with the wonders of the new normal.

Summary of Tuners

At this writing, Amazon.com shows five pages, each with about fifteen different tuners for a total of seventy-five tuners of all kinds now on the market. The choices start with a simple device with four joined tuned pipes into which one can blow to produce a desired pitch to match. This inexpensive pitch pipe is most popular and probably the only pitch pipe necessary for a beginning student. The advantage of this simple product is that it requires the student to listen to and think of pitch instead of relying on visual aids to tune. Music is an auditory art and, consequently, every avenue that fosters training the ear to hear and the mind to think sound is another step toward success. The next level would be the chromatic version described above. All the extra notes are of no use in tuning a four-string instrument, though having them available should there be a need cannot hurt.

Human beings possess every level of pitch discrimination from perfect to tone deaf. For those with excellent pitch discrimination, an electronic tuner that produces a pitch without visual enhancement and eliminates the need to blow into a pitch pipe can provide an adequate tuning experience. For those who are weak in pitch discrimination, a visual aid or screen showing how the sound being produced relates to the actual pitch needed can be an excellent learning tool. As the student learns visually to discriminate pitches, s/he can, by concentrating on listening to a pitch while seeing it, gradually improve pitch discrimination.

Fine Tuners

Fine tuners are attached to the tailpiece of an instrument and are available in at least six different forms. As the name implies, their function is to tune the strings up or down in very fine increments to facilitate tuning accuracy. After a string is tuned by turning the peg, the final step would be to fine-tune that string by turning a small screw that is part of the fine tuner mechanism. The Suzuki model fine tuners are independent tuners that are attached directly to a string (Fig. 8.8).

Figure 8.8 Suzuki Fine Tuner

Another style fine tuner attaches to the tailpiece and the string is then connected directly to the fine tuner (Fig. 8.9).

Figure 8.9 Fine Tuners Attached to the Tailpiece

If a fine tuner is desired for each of the four strings, one can find tailpieces with four built-in fine tuners (Fig 8.10). The tuners are actually part of the tailpiece and the string is attached to the fine tuner instead of directly to the tailpiece.

Figure 8.10 Tailpiece

Electric Pickups

Chapter 3 provides a detailed explanation of pickups of all types for all the instruments of the violin family.

Peg Treatment

Slipping and stuck pegs are a chronic problem for violins, violas, and cellos, all instruments with wooden, wedge-shaped pegs. Since the wood of the peg box and the pegs, each a different kind of wood, expand and contract at different rates, the pegs on these instruments can lose their holding power. There are several products on the market to deal with this problem. The oldest cure is peg compound, a heavy paste-like product usually brown in color that is applied to the pegs to prevent sticking or slipping pegs (Fig. 8.11).

Figure 8.11 Paste Peg Treatment

This product works reasonably well but, in order to apply it, one must remove the string from the peg, remove the peg, apply the compound to the peg, work the peg into the peg hole to distribute the compound, and then replace the string into the hole in the peg. This is particularly frustrating because as a result of being wound on the peg, the end of the original string is now curled up making rethreading it difficult.

A more contemporary solution to peg problems, also with a proven record of success, is Peg Drops (Fig. 8.12). This product is a liquid compound which requires the user to simply loosen the peg with the string in place, apply one drop to the peg at the two points where it comes in contact with the peg box and then slid the peg back into place.

Figure 8.12 Liquid Peg Treatment

Bow Hair

Over time the hair on any bow will suffer from rosin buildup and begin to attract dirt from handling and the environment. The usual solution for this problem was to re-hair the bow. The Bow Hair Rejuvenation Kit (Fig. 8.13) consists of a liquid bow cleaning solvent, a cloth with which to apply the solvent, a comb to straighten out the hairs after the solvent dries, and a liquid rosin solution to apply to the hair at the end of the cleaning process. Follow the instructions. It works.

Figure 8.13 Bow Hair Treatment

Strings

A search on Google produced fifty-seven different brands of violin E strings. Therefore, this writer will not comment on or recommend any strings by brand name.

A number of different materials are currently being used to manufacture strings. Among the most common are gut, steel, perlon (a type of stranded plastic fiber), nylon, silk, chromium/steel, and gold. With the exception of the gold strings, all the other products can be used as a core for strings that are then wrapped with aluminum, chromium, or silver. This process can be used for all strings except the violin E string which, because of its high pitch, does not require the acoustical enhancement provided by wrapping.

Each type of string construction produces a different sound and can alter the overall tone quality of an instrument, making the choice of strings a matter worthy of great consideration. One may elect to brighten or darken the tone quality of an instrument or alter the tone projection or amplitude by selecting the string material that will produce the desired effect.

When striving to achieve a particular sound, one must consider the timbre of the instrument being strung and anticipate how that instrument will respond to each type of string. Unfortunately, there are no definitive prescriptions for making this determination but there are some general guidelines which may facilitate making the choice. Within these broad parameters, a player can engage in trial and error experimentation to arrive at the combination of string and instrument that will produce an acceptable sound.

Steel or steel core strings are most durable, produce the most aggressive, brightest sound, stay in tune longer, and are generally prescribed for use by beginning players. Because of steel's strength, the strings can be made with less material thereby increasing the production of upper partials in a given pitch while improving bowing response.

Gut strings are made of the entrails of animals. These strings produce a more mellow sound, but since they react to changes in temperature and humidity, they are highly susceptible to pitch problems and tend to break more easily. Gut core strings, which are wound with silver or aluminum, retain the characteristics of the pure gut but tend to have a fuller sound and somewhat greater durability. It is the winding on the gut core that allows the core to be thinner and therefore more responsive.

Synthetic core strings are made with nylon or other manufactured substances as a core. The synthetic core is intended to reproduce the positive attributes of a gut core string but is stronger than gut, does not react greatly to temperature and humidity changes, and tends to stay in tune longer. Strings manufactured in this fashion produce a brighter, more aggressive sound than gut strings.

Tension

A string's tension is the product of its length, mass, and the pitch to which it is tuned. The balance of these factors combined will determine the quality of the sound being produced and the ease of response the string will offer the player. As the thickness of a string increases, the tension required to tune that string will increase and it will be less responsive to bowing. Higher tension strings can produce a louder sound than the lower tension strings.

Strings are produced in different thicknesses. They are categorized by some manufacturers as light, medium, or heavy. Others use a proprietary system of numbers to identify their string sizes. The terms light, medium, and heavy offer sound and bowing responses commensurate with their labels. Lighter strings respond easily and allow the player to produce a wider spectrum of more sensitive sounds but with less volume. Heavy tension strings produce a fuller dynamic in both tone and volume but they do so at the expense of bowing response and flexibility. Medium labeled strings strike a balance between the two extremes. There are, however, no industry-wide standards for this nomenclature so there can be significant variations between similar labels from different manufacturers. A comparison trial of same tension strings from several different manufacturers would be the way to decide on the best string for an individual player.

Strings are constructed with either a loop end, ball end, or knot end which is inserted in the keyhole-shaped hole in the tailpiece or directly onto a fine tuner. The loop and ball ends are usually found on most strings whereas the knot end is used for gut strings without windings. See Figure 7.3 in chapter 7 for an image of those string ends.

Chin Rests

A chin rest is included with any violin or viola rental or purchase. Since there is probably a model chin rest to meet every individual's needs, it is recommended that a new player begin by using the chin rest that comes with the instrument. If that chin rest is found to be uncomfortable, the next step would be to visit a music store that specializes in violins and violas and try the patience of the salesperson by trying all the chin rests available. They come in different sizes, shapes, and in configurations that can place the player's chin at any point on the instrument from the far left to the center over the tailpiece.

The many varieties offered are made of materials such as Bakelite, ebony, rosewood, assorted plastics, and practically any other material that can be formed into the required shape. The choice of shape is totally a matter of individual preference and should be decided upon on the basis of the comfort and ease of playing it provides for the player. The material from which a chin rest is made does not influence its effectiveness but can affect the price and so one's budget should be the determining factor in making a decision. The following are some examples of the many different shapes available (Fig. 8.14).

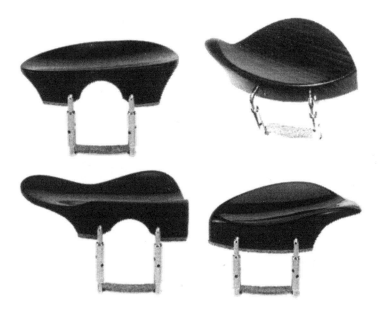

Figure 8.14 Different Style Chin Rests

The Chinbow is an adjustable chinrest (Fig. 8.15). The cup section made of a soft product is movable and can be raised or lowered and swiveled a full 360 degrees to any position desired.

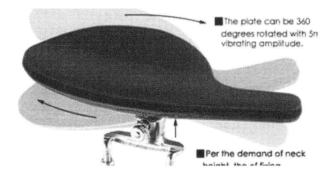

Figure 8.15 Adjustable Chin Rest

Chin Rest Pads

Chin rest pads are intended to increase the level of comfort for the player. As is the case with all other accessories, these pads are available in many forms and sizes. There are corduroy pockets that slip over the chin rest, gel-filled pads that stick on to the chin rest, various felt pads that attach with Velcro, and an assortment of variations on the above (Fig. 8.16). Chin rest pads are not a necessary item and should be considered only if one feels the need.

GelRest   Chin Cozy

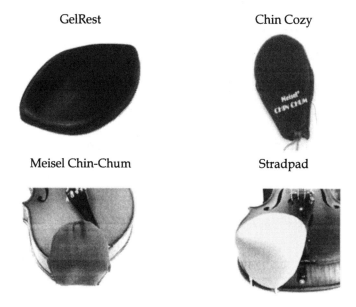

Meisel Chin-Chum   Stradpad

Figure 8.16 Chin Rest Pads

Shoulder Rests

The distance between one's shoulder and chin, i.e., the length of one's neck is another unique physical characteristic that must be accommodated for when playing a violin or viola. Although not a necessity, a shoulder rest can help a player maintain the proper playing position by supporting the instrument. Using a properly fitted shoulder rest can increase the support of the instrument by the chin and shoulder thereby releasing that burden from the left hand, allowing it more ease of motion to shift positions.

Studies have indicated that shoulder rests can interfere with the vibration occurring on the back of an instrument. This effect has given rise to some deliberation regarding the value of using a shoulder rest. Many highly renowned performers do not use one; however, the question then remains how different the effect of the device is from that of one's shoulder which also muffles a certain amount of vibration.

A number of shoulder rests are available to accommodate individual needs in that area. The following are some of the more popular model shoulder rests that have been accepted by the violin and viola playing public over the years.

A brace supported by legs is a common design produced by several manufacturers all of whom make slight modifications to a shapely foam-padded bar with adjustable height legs (Fig. 8.17). This model is manufactured by Kun, who offers six variations, Viva La Musica with three types, along with Wolf, Resonans, Bonmusica, Mach One, Everest, Stowmaster, and Pede Elegante, all offering their versions of the same basic configuration. All of these are available in many sizes for both the violin and viola.

Figure 8.17 Shoulder Rest

Play-on-air is an inflatable pillow that comes in different sizes (Fig 8.18). It is filled with air by blowing into a tube much like that used in a beach ball. These come in five different models varying in height and size.

Figure 8.18 Play-on-Air

Poehland is one of the older shoulder rest models. This device is a half-circular, fabric-covered firm pad that is attached to the end button of the violin by a leather strip and the lower bout edge of the violin or viola body by a combination of a leather strip and a rubber band (Fig. 8.19).

Figure 8.19 Firm Shoulder Pad

The Zaret shoulder rest is a very inexpensive, shaped foam pad suitable for violin and viola (Fig. 8.20).

Figure 8.20 Foam Shoulder Pad

A modified rectangular-shaped piece of foam rubber which is held on to the violin by a rubber-band can be fabricated at practically no cost.

Mutes

A mute is a device placed on a musical instrument to modify the natural sound being produced (Fig. 8.21). On a string instrument, this modification is accomplished by restricting the vibrations that are carried into the body of the instrument through the bridge. The most common mute used for a string instrument is a three or four prong device made of wood which is placed on the top of the bridge thereby restricting or muting the vibrations. Two other mute types that accomplish the same goal are a rubber disk with two openings for the strings and a wire configuration with a plastic arch. These are also attached to the top of the bridge to mute the tone. Mutes for the different instruments of the violin family differ only in size. Larger instruments use larger mutes.

Figure 8.21 Different Mutes

Cases

Violin and Viola Cases

Violin and viola cases are made in a shape similar to that of the instrument, in oblong shapes, and in half moon shapes. The material used to make the case can be wood, plastic, or any other combination of material that can be formed into the needed shape. Shaped cases made of molded plastic are usually the least expensive and most durable for beginning students (Fig. 8.22). Better quality shaped cases are made of wood or other pressed material that is covered with fabric in various colors.

Figure 8.22 Molded Plastic Violin Case

Oblong cases are constructed using the same basic materials used for the shaped cases (Fig. 8.23). The difference is in the shape and size of the case. Oblong cases can be made with a hard thermo-plastic or fiberglass exterior or a fabric covered wooden exterior. They are larger than the shaped case with a larger interior carrying capacity. Often these cases include a pocket built onto the exterior fabric cover that can be used to carry music and other personal items.

Figure 8.23 Oblong Cases

The details of the construction of the interior of either shaped or oblong cases can range from a simple felt covering with a small box at the scroll end to house rosin to the most elaborate plush velour padding imaginable. These cases can include an attached blanket for the violin, four satin-lined brackets for four bows, tubes to carry extra strings, a large box for rosin, a shoulder rest, tuning device, and whatever else one wishes to carry. Both the shaped and oblong upgraded cases can also include a suspension system designed to support the violin at points of strength while protecting the more sensitive parts of the instrument. The violin is literally suspended in air so that the body and bridge do not come in contact with any part of the case (Fig. 8.24).

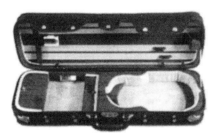

Figure 8.24 Suspension Case

Half-moon shaped cases are a recent addition to the case market (Fig. 8.25). Made for violins and violas, this model has all the features of the oblong case above but contained within a half moon shape.

Figure 8.25 Half-Moon Case

Cello Cases

Cello cases are available with a hard shell or a soft fabric cello-shaped bag. The choice sounds simple but, as is the case (oops, a third unintended pun) with all things musical, that simple choice is complicated by the many variations available in those two forms.

Most hard shell cases are made to fit most full size cellos. However, there are exceptions, and so a fitting is a must. Figure 8.26 shows the exterior of a hard shell case. These cases are available in many price ranges determined by the degree of refinement of the case. Wheels are one refinement which is often overlooked but highly recommended. The total weight of a cello, its accessories, music, and case can be a significant burden to transport for even a short distance.

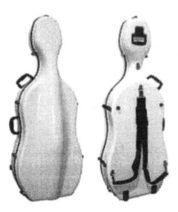

Figure 8.26 Hard Shell Cello Case

Hard shell cello cases are made with different interiors ranging from a basic felt lining to the most elaborate plush design. Figure 8.27 shows an interior with padding in appropriate locations to help protect the instrument from any potential damage from a severe jolt.

Figure 8.27 Hard Shell Cello Case Interior

Cello bags can also be obtained in many forms from a simple shaped canvas bag to one that is heavily padded. These are made from various fabrics and have a variety of different pockets to hold the bow, music, a stand, and whatever else is needed by the player. Figure 8.28 is an example of two levels of soft padded cello bags.

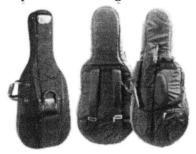

Figure 8.28   Padded Shaped Cello Bags

Double Bass Cases

Double bass cases follow the same formula as do cello cases with both hard and soft versions available. For the double bass hard shell case, wheels are almost an imperative because of the weight of the instrument, its assorted accessories, and the case itself. A soft bag is lighter than the hard shell model and does have handles to facilitate carrying. If the soft bag is the choice, it is recommended that a bass dolly or wheel be added to the package to facilitate moving the instrument. Figure 8.29 illustrates a bass wheel which can be put in place of the endpin and pair of wheels that can be strapped on to the instrument.

Figure 8.29 Double Bass Wheels

Figure 8.30 illustrates a front and back view of a hard shell double bass case. The exterior is made of glass fiber with a plush velour interior suspension system to keep the instrument safe from being jolted. Note the built-in wheels and numerous handles on the case.

Figure 8.30 Hard Shell Double Bass Case

Figure 8.31 illustrates a soft cover well-padded case with wheels, carrying straps, and a back-pack-carrying strap to aid in transportation. This style case also contains several pouches and compartments for bows and other accessories.

Figure 8.31 Padded Soft Double Bass Case

The Gollihur Music website contains an illustration of the measurements for the soft cases they sell (Fig. 8.32A). The website also shows a double bass divided into sections (Fig. 8.32B) with an accompanying chart showing the dimensions of the various parts of the instrument. This is an excellent aid for one who is searching for a case. Take the chart on the search before you lug the bass.

Kay brand basses are unique in their dimensions. This is another example of the need for one to be sure to try the instrument in the case under consideration before the sale is final. Double basses are the most inconsistent of all the instruments in the violin family for size and shape. Keep this in mind as you proceed in the search for a case.

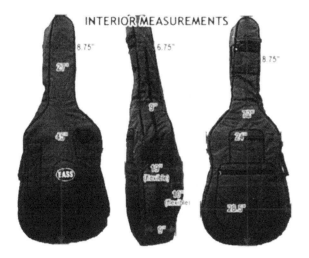

Figure 8.32A Gollihur Measured Double Bass Bags

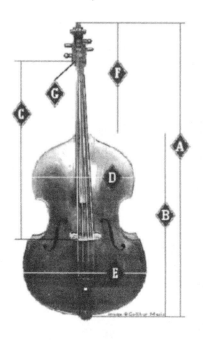

		4/4	3/4	3/4 Kay	1/2	1/4
A	Full Height bottom of body to scroll	74.8	71.6	71.6	65.7	61.4
B	Body Height bottom to shoulder	45.7	43.7	43.7	40.2	37.4
C	Scale Length nut to bridge	43.3	41.3	41.5	38	35.4
D	Upper Bout Width	21.3	20.3	20.25	18.7	17.3
E	Lower Bout Width	26.8	25.6	26.5	23.6	21.9
F	Scroll to Shoulder	29.1	27.9	28	25.5	24.0
G	Width at Nut	1.8	1.7	1.6	1.6	1.5
Reproduced with the permission of Gollihur Music.						

Figure 8.32B Double Bass Sizing Chart

Hygrometers & Humidifiers

It is essential that a string instrument be housed in a moderate climate. As stated previously, any extreme temperature and/or humidity can cause severe damage to the instrument. A hygrometer measures the level of humidity within a managed space. Keeping this device in a case can be a valuable aid in monitoring the humidity. Should that hygrometer indicate an excessively dry climate, the next step would be to install a humidifier in the case. Available are hygrometers specifically designed to be used in an instrument case (Fig. 8.33). Of course, any hygrometer that will fit conveniently in a case can be used.

Figure 8.33 Hygrometers

Should the climate inside a case be too dry, case humidifiers are available in many forms. These are recommended by many luthiers for use in dry climates and during the winter in colder climates where indoor heat is used. Humidifiers are basic water-holding devices of various designs.

A Dampit case humidifier (Fig. 8.34) is a perforated rubber tube filled with absorbent material that holds water. When an instrument is not in use, the Dampit tube soaked in water is inserted into the body of the instrument through the F hole. The Dampit is removed when the instrument is in use. A humidity-measuring color chart that indicates the level of ambient humidity is included with the Dampit kit.

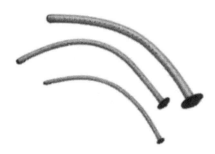

Figure 8.34 Three Different Size Dampits

The Stretto is another item that can be used to maintain a consistent degree of humidity within a case (Fig. 8.35). This unit is essentially a perforated plastic box that contains an absorbent material. The material is soaked in water and, if left in a case, is said to be effective for up to two weeks.

Figure 8.35 Stretto Violin Humidifier

There are numerous other humidifiers. They all hold water in some way and claim to achieve the same end, which is to maintain an acceptable level of humidity within a case. Figure 8.36 shows three different types of humidifiers now on the market.

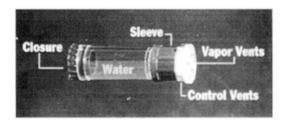

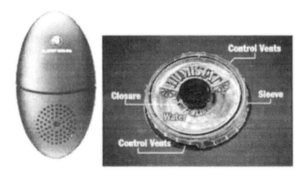

Figure 8.36 Three Different Humidifiers

Music Stands

A music stand is a very important aid to playing an instrument. Correct posture and playing position are essential to successful performance on any instrument. The recommended traditional seating, standing, and playing positions evolved as a time-tested result of adjusting these positions to achieve the best playing results. When one reads music while playing, the music must be placed at a distance suitable for the individual to see it comfortably, while bowing the instrument freely. Thus, we have the music stand.

Music stands are sold in three basic designs with numerous variations for each. There are stands that fold, those that are rigid or non-folding, and tabletop versions. The folding stand or sheet music stand (Fig. 8.37) is very useful for a beginning student. It is lightweight, totally portable, and very inexpensive. Folding stands can also be purchased with a carrying case for even more convenient portability. A caveat to this low cost mobility is found in the stand's fragility and some degree of instability. These stands can easily be knocked over and the lightweight parts can be bent out of shape.

Figure 8.37 Folding Music Stand

The rigid design stand (Fig. 8.38) sometimes referred to as concert, stage, or orchestra music stand, is not convenient to carry, usually quite heavy, and intended to be used most often in one particular place. They are more expensive than the folding stand but are very stable, able to hold a significant amount of music, and are practically indestructible. The cost of these stands usually ranges from two to four times that of a folding stand.

Figure 8.38 Concert Stand

Should the budget permit, one can purchase every degree of elaboration on the basic design from contemporary to Baroque style at costs that can run into hundreds of dollars (Fig. 8.39).

Figure 8.39 Baroque Style Music Stand

A tabletop stand is small, highly portable, does not have legs, and is lightweight and inexpensive. It can be placed on any stable surface and allows complete flexibility. The caveat here is that, should it be positioned on a conventional tabletop, the music could be too low for a player in standing position to see while maintaining a proper playing position. This stand may work for one who is playing in the sitting position. Figure 8.40 shows three models of table top stands: the first a decorative model, the second a folding design, and the third a concert style.

Figure 8.40 Tabletop Stands

Some students elect to place their music on a piano music stand. This is not recommended since the stand lacks portability and restricts control of the distance and height the music can be placed from the player. Depending on the piano, the position may also be too low to allow for a proper playing position.

Additional Cello Accessories

Rock Stop

The rock stop is a device used to prevent a cello endpin from slipping. The rock stop also protects the flooring from being damaged. One style can be some form of rubber based shape with an indentation in which to place the endpin (Fig. 8.41). The rubber base adheres to the floor and is less likely to slip.

Figure 8.41 Rock Stop

Two other types use the player's chair leg as an anchor (Fig. 8.42), the leg in the larger hole and the endpin in the smaller hole.

Figure 8.42 Endpin Holders

Endpins can be replaced by an experienced technician with little difficulty. Should the original endpin on a cello not be satisfactory, one can find a variety of sizes, lengths, and configurations to suit the individual's needs. Figure 8.43 shows an angular endpin and an extended length model with a rubber tip.

Figure 8.43 Endpins

Rubber tips (Fig. 8.44) are available for easy installation on any endpin.

Figure 8.44 End Pin Rubber Tip

Cello Bridge Height Adjustor
See double bass accessories Figures 8.51, 52, and 53.

Cello Stands
Cello stands are available in many configurations and at all price levels. The style selected should be decided upon according to the need for flexibility and mobility and to suit the decor of the room in which it will be used. Figure 8.45 shows a box design which is not particularly portable but is probably the most secure stand for a cello.

Figure 8.45 Box Cello Stand

Figure 8.46 shows a more decorative movable stand but perhaps a bit less stable than the box style.

Figure 8.46 Movable Cello Stand

Figure 8.47 illustrates the most portable of cello stands. It is light weight, adjustable, and offers a secure padded neck brace on which a cello can rest.

Figure 8.47 Portable Cello Stand

Wolf Tone Eliminator

A wolf tone is an upper partial or overtone that is produced artificial-
ly by the symbiotic interaction of a tone with the natural resonance of the
body of the instrument being played. The result is a sound similar to that
of a wolf's howl. Wolf tones can occur on almost any instrument. It is
most commonly noticed on string instruments and most especially on the
cello and double bass. Wolf tones can be muffled by interfering with the
runaway vibrations. By placing a wolf tone eliminator between the bridge
and tailpiece on the offending string, the objectionable sound is muted.
Figure 8.48 shows two types of wolf tone eliminators individually and in
position on a cello.

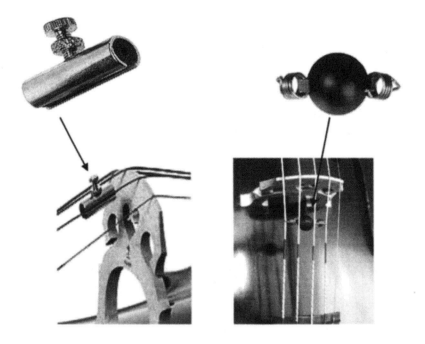

Figure 8.48 Wolf Tone Eliminators

Additional Double Bass Accessories

Double Bass Bib

A double bass bib (Fig. 8.49) is a product designed to protect the finish of an instrument from scratches and the wear which can occur as the body of the bass is in contact with the player's body. A common problem is caused by the player's belt buckle scratching the instrument. Constant contact with the player's clothing can act as an abrasive, rubbing the finish off the bass. Bibs also contain various compartments and pockets which are handy for the player to keep small items such as rosin, a peg winder, pitch pipe or tuner, and the like.

Figure 8.49 Double Bass Bib

String Winder

Tuning a double bass usually requires at most a few turns of the machine head gear. However, changing a string is another case. Removing and replacing a string can require as many as 150 turns down and then as many up. The invention of the string winder (Fig. 8.50), a little known but very helpful device, assists in easing the problem. The String Winder is available in both hand operated and machine operated models. Which one to select would depend on how often one changes a string.

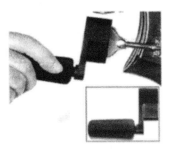

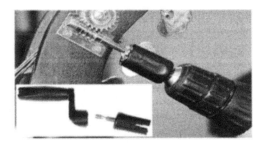

Figure 8.50 String Winder

Double Bass Bridge Adjustor

A bridge adjustor facilitates the raising and lowering of a bridge. With changes in climate come changes in the height of the belly of many instruments. To accommodate this phenomenon, string players keep several bridges of different heights which they change as needed. Because of the large size of the double bass bridges and the thickness of their legs, it is possible to install an adjustor which will allow one to raise or lower the bridge with a turn of a screw. These adjusters have one end with a smooth surface, the other end with a threaded surface, and a wheel in the middle (Fig. 8.51). These two units can be installed in a bridge as pictured in Figure 8.52.

Figure 8.51 Adjustable Bridge Screws

Figure 8.52 Adjustable Bridge Parts

The final product is a bridge which can be lowered or raised with the turn of a screw (Fig. 8.53).

Figure 8.53 Adjustable Bridge Complete

Double Bass Stands

All musical instrument accessories are available in an infinite and ever changing variety. Such is the case with double bass stands. Figure 8.54 shows two kinds of stands currently on the market. It is recommended that an interested buyer start a search on line because this type of specialized equipment is not usually kept in stock in the average music store. Once one finds a few examples of stands that might be acceptable, phone calls to the larger stores or online contacts can be used to ascertain availability.

Figure 8.54 Double Bass Stands

Bow Quivers

A bow quiver is designed to store a bow when it is not in use. During performance intermissions or extended rehearsals, there are periods when a bow will be left unattended. During these times, bows are damaged. The bow quiver provides a safe, temporary place in which to leave a bow unattended.

Quivers can be made of any suitable product from the finest leather to some form of plastic. Figure 8.55 illustrates three different quivers.

Figure 8.55 Bow Quivers

Conclusion

This chapter has introduced the reader to the various categories of accessories and some varieties within each category. Further research by the consumer will show hundreds of additional variants. The introduction to this chapter states that musical instrument accessories fall into the categories of those that are necessary, those that significantly facilitate the playing and maintenance of an instrument, and those that are luxuries. These three categories are not divided by strict rules. What may be one person's luxury could well be considered by another to be a necessity. As is usually the case in the music world, the decision is unique to the individual.

Chapter 9
How String Instruments Compare
to Each Other

As explained in chapter 2, How They Work, the violin, viola, cello, and double bass are very similar in their design, acoustics, and construction. They share many playing techniques and fingering patterns that make it possible for one to double and even triple on any of these instruments. This chapter will show the similarities and differences in the four instruments of the violin family.

The bows and the holding and playing positions for the violin and viola are similar so that switching from one to the other would only be a matter of adjusting to the different sizes. This size adjustment is also true for the cello and the French style double bass bows. These two also share the same holding and playing positions but are drawn across the instruments at waist level instead of at chin level for the violin and viola. The differences are in the size of the stick and the frog. The German style double bass bow is the only exception in that it is held with a full hand grip. See chapter 2 for additional details.

Tuning the Instruments

The violin, viola, and cello all have wedge-shaped wooden pegs which are forced into holes in the peg box and so all use the same tuning process. See chapter 2 for additional details. The double bass uses a worm and gear system to accommodate the tension of the thicker strings. The tuning process is still the same as it is with the other instruments with the positive exception that the worm and gear system eliminates the problem the other instruments have of slipping pegs.

The Open Strings

The strings on violin and viola are tuned in fifths. These instruments share the tuning of three of their four strings. The exception is on the viola where the lowest string is tuned to C, a fifth below the lowest string on the violin which is G. Comparing the two staves below, it is easy to see the similarities (Fig. 9.1 & 9.2). The other difference is found in viola music which is written in the movable C clef to more easily accommodate the range of the notes played on that instrument. By using the movable C clef, the violist will have more of the notes in the viola playing range written on the staff as opposed to on ledger lines. One method used by some violinists when reading viola music is to visualize a written note as being one higher while sounding an octave lower.

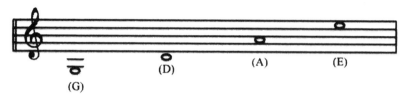

Figure 9.1 Violin Open Strings

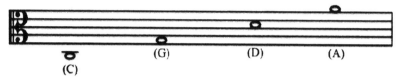

Figure 9.2 Viola Open Strings
(Movable C clef represents middle C.)

When transitioning down to the cello, the reader will note that it is tuned to the same notes as the viola but one octave lower. Also, cello notation is written in the bass clef (Fig. 9.3).

Figure 9.3 Cello Open Strings

The double bass, also written in the bass clef, is tuned as a violin turned upside down. The violin strings top to bottom are E, A, D, and G, whereas the double bass strings top to bottom are G, D, A, and E (Fig. 9.4). This inversion results in the double bass being the only instrument of the four to be tuned in fourths instead of fifths.

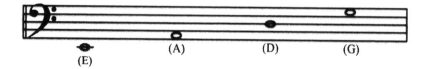

Figure 9.4 Double Bass Open Strings

Additionally, the double bass sounds an octave below the written note so the double bass's highest string written G (the same as the lowest string on the violin) sounds one octave lowers than that.

To summarize, the relationship of the four instruments' open strings to one another, the violin shares three strings with the viola, the cello is a duplicate of the viola but an octave lower, and the double bass is the violin upside down, an octave lower in print and two octaves lower in sound. Assembled, they represent the four voices of a chorus — the violin being the soprano, the viola the alto, the cello the tenor, and the double bass the bass voice.

The Violin and Viola

Because the fingering patterns for the violin and viola are almost identical, it is not particularly difficult for one to transition from one to the other. Both instruments have seven positions on each string which progress in whole steps, with easy access to produce half step progressions. The switch is a matter of adjusting to the difference in the size of the instruments, to the lower C string on the viola, and to the C clef used for viola music. Figures 9.5 and 9.6 show the violin and viola fingering charts side by side for a comparison. Note that the fingering patterns are the same and the only difference is one string.

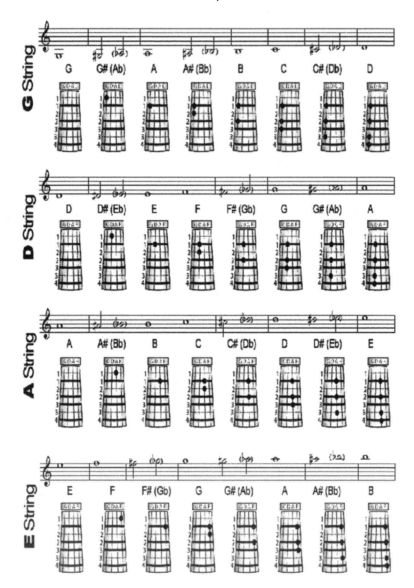

Figure 9.5 Basic Violin Fingering Chart

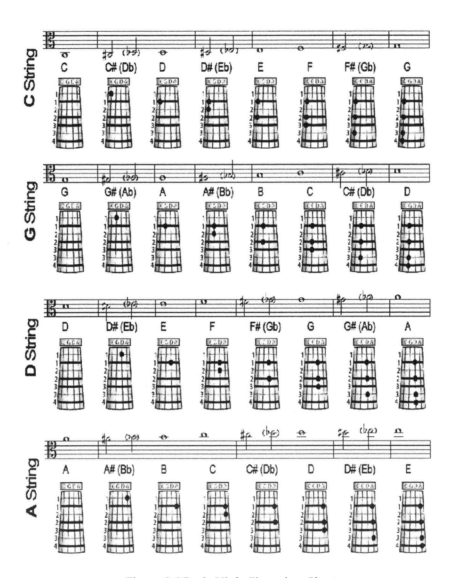

Figure 9.6 Basic Viola Fingering Chart

The Cello

Switching from a violin or viola to a cello requires a somewhat greater adjustment in playing position, bowing technique, and reading music in a different clef. However, they are still in the same family, using the basic concepts of producing sound by bowing or plucking and changing the length of the vibrating strings by pressing them on a fingerboard.

One plays the cello while seated, holding the instrument between the knees at a position just below the C bout. Bow hand position is similar to that of the violin and viola in that the bow is held in the same manner as both these smaller instruments. It differs in that the cello strings are the reverse of those of the violin and viola with the highest string on those instruments on the player's right side and the cello's highest string on the left side.

When one plays a cello, the bow runs parallel to the floor at about waist height as the player is seated. This situation is very different from bowing a violin or viola and so the transition from violin and viola to the cello is not as smooth as one between the two smaller instruments and may require a bit more effort to reach a level of comfort.

Fingering patterns on a cello (Fig. 9.7) differ from those of the violin and viola in that the cello fingering progresses by half steps, the pattern being ½, 1st, 2nd, 2½, 3rd, 3½, 4th, 5th, 5½, 6th, 6½, and 7th. Each of these positions progresses by half steps up to the seventh position. Whereas violinist and violist can play five half steps in each position, the cellist can play only three half steps. There are no half positions for the first and fourth positions because of the natural half step between E and F, and B and C in the diatonic scale.

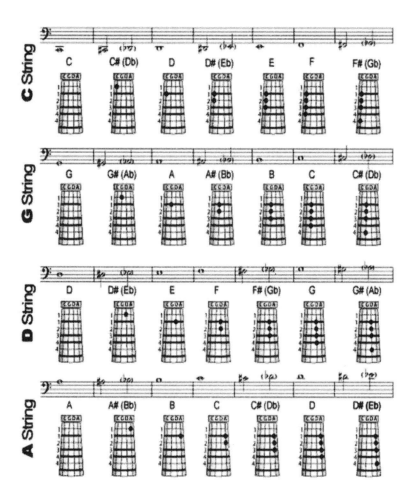

Figure 9.7 Basic Cello Fingering Chart

The Double Bass

As the instruments of the family increase in size, transitioning from one to the other increases in difficulty. Jumping from a violin to a double bass is certainly more difficult than from a violin to a viola; however, there are sufficient similarities to make it feasible if not immediate. Going from a cello to a double bass is easier because of the similarity of playing position. The instruments are both standing on the ground and bowing perpendicular to the floor. The one aspect common to all four instruments is that of holding the bow, assuming the double bass bow is French style.

Fingering for the double bass (Figure 9.8) follows a slightly different pattern since its larger size requires a greater spread between notes. Also, the ring finger is never used alone but is used in conjunction with the pinky. Used individually, they both generally lack strength.

The pattern for the positions on the double bass, starting from an open string is: ½, 1st, 2nd, 2½, 3rd, 3½, 4th, 5th, 5½, 6th, 6½, and 7th. Each of these positions progresses by half steps up to the seventh position. The double bass player is restricted to playing only three half steps in a position because the third and fourth fingers are used in combination. There are no half positions for the first and fourth positions because of the natural half step between E and F, and B and C in the diatonic scale.

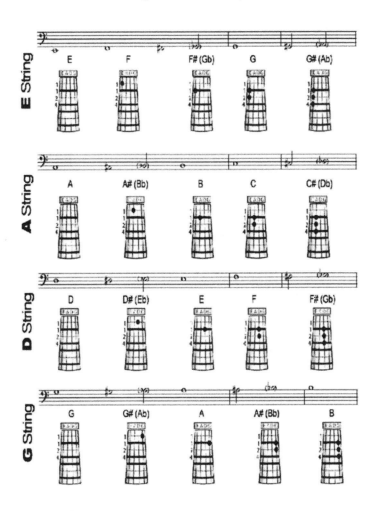

Figure 9.8 Basic Double Bass Fingering Chart

Chapter 10
Learning to Play

Choosing a Music Teacher

Choosing a music teacher is certainly the most important decision one must make in the study process. As is the case with everything in life, there are functioning teachers who rank from the best to the worst in teaching skills, knowledge, personality, and general gestalt. The choice is, at best, a gamble. This chapter will help in making a decision.

When an individual played the first sounds on whatever might have been the first sound producing item for him or her, one might say with some confidence that the player showed someone what s/he did and then how to do it. That was the first music lesson, a bit simplistic but quite a reasonable assumption. "Look, Charley, this thing makes sounds". "How did you do that?" "This is how." We have since come a long way in the evolution of musical instruments and the methods used to teach one how to play them.

The publishing world abounds with method books for every instrument. The questions are: which method to use and who shall be the teacher to use it? These are questions almost impossible to answer with any degree of confidence. In the perfect world, one would seek the advice and counsel of someone knowledgeable in the field of music education who has no personal agenda, will not benefit from the decision, and has had professional and personal experience with the teacher under consideration. Not an easy bill to fill. Unfortunately, this is not a perfect world, so what would be the best next step?

A successful music teacher must be equipped with an uplifting personality, knowledge, musical talent, teaching skills, an ability to communicate easily, and a love for the job that results in a complete commitment to the profession.

Personality

The relationship between a music teacher and student can be the most important part of the learning process. The student will be visiting with the teacher on a weekly basis or possibly more often. With that in mind, consider how it would feel spending an hour or more with someone who was not particularly pleasant to be with. Not an experience to look forward to each week. Should likability be a deciding factor in teacher selection? Yes! But it should not be the only factor. An equally important question is whether the teacher can teach. How does one find out about that?

Teaching Skills

The most effective way to judge a music teacher's teaching skills is by observing the teacher in action and evaluating his or her student's achievements. Watching a great teacher in action followed by an equally good performance by his or her students is an indication that something positive must be happening to achieve that end. To implement this evaluation procedure, it would be necessary to have access to the teacher's lessons and students' performance. In a music school, such access is commonly provided on a regular basis either in the form of periodic public events or by appointment. When dealing with a private teacher who provides only one-on-one instruction, access may be less likely. In that case, inquiry by word of mouth through the students and their parents would be an alternative approach.

Education and Professional Experience

Checking a teacher's credentials, degrees, and training should not be particularly difficult. Usually, those are made public in the teacher's biography or advertising. In many cases, Googling the teacher's name will produce all the information needed and in some cases more than the teacher wants to be known. The fact that an individual has a stellar education with many degrees is laudable; however, such credentials do not necessarily guarantee that the individual will be an outstanding teacher. A great performer with a long list of credentials might allow those achievements to inflate his or her ego to the point where it interferes with the teaching process on a fundamental level. Such a teacher would probably better serve advanced students.

In the final analysis, teaching is not only a science but also an art. It is one that requires a balance of all the above attributes possessed by a puppet master so to speak in the form of an individual who is capable of pulling the right string at the right time under a given student interaction to achieve the best results.

The Methods

SheetMusicPlus.Com, an accredited business with the Better Business Bureau, advertises 264 violin methods, 135 viola methods, 219 cello methods, and 65 double bass methods. So much for reviewing or recommending any one of those methods. Their popularity ranges from minimal to great, but it is possible that the least popular method could be the best for a particular teacher/student match. The most widely sold method is that which was developed by Dr. Shinichi Suzuki.

Shinichi Suzuki (1898-1998)

Shinichi Suzuki, born in Nagoya, Japan in 1898, was the son of a luthier, and owner of one of the largest violin factories. Shinichi, at first a self-taught violinist, eventually studied with some of the greatest violin teachers of that time and became the conductor of the Tokyo String Orchestra. It was during that period that he theorized that it would be possible for young people to learn to play a musical instrument in the same manner that they learn to speak.

The Suzuki Method

The Suzuki Method of teaching music is a departure from the traditional methods that have been used for centuries. It reverses the early learning process in which one is introduced to an individual note written on a page and simultaneously learns to play that note. The Suzuki Method starts the student by observing, listening, and immediately playing without notation and with minimal technical instruction. Dr. Suzuki theorized that it should be possible for one to learn music from early childhood just as a young child learns a language. By hearing, listening, and associating what is being heard with something tangible, one can apply those three activities to an undertaking that will produce a desired result. One does not learn the written word or the principles of grammar as one learns to speak. That understanding all follows after having first learned to speak a language. So, why not use the same paradigm to learn music? Dr. Suzuki did, and it worked!

In the mid-twentieth century, Dr. Suzuki, using his new method of teaching the violin in a music school in Japan, began to attract the attention of teachers from other parts of the world. As interest grew, these teachers visited the small school in Japan to learn about the new method and a group of students from that school traveled to the United States and Europe to demonstrate it. By the mid 1970s the music world had been introduced to what is now known as the Suzuki Method of teaching the violin eventually to include the four instruments of the violin family. Many of the students of that method have gone on to become professional performers and teachers using the Suzuki Method, which is now accepted worldwide as a driving force in teaching the violin, viola, cello, and double bass.

The language learning process begins from birth with exposure to words as a result of normal social interaction. As a child begins to use words in speech, a corrective intervention occurs by adults to help in the

words as a result of normal social interaction. As a child begins to use words in speech, a corrective intervention occurs by adults to help in the formation of proper sentence structure. Ultimately, reading printed words already in use and the formal study of grammar complete the cycle.

Following the same learning pattern, a child exposed to music from birth subliminally processes the sounds. It is then possible to channel those imbedded audio experiences into actions that will reproduce these sounds on an instrument. This application can begin at whatever age (even as early as two years old) is appropriate for the individual. Interaction with peer groups is used to reinforce the development just as one would normally experience with speech.

This activity is one of learning to play on an instrument what one has heard, is hearing, and has processed. A child speaks before seeing words on a page and so he or she should play before seeing notes on a page. The objective is to postpone the theoretical aspects of music study to a point where the player has reasonable facility with the instrument. Almost all attention is given to the mechanics of playing and to ear training, both of which are essential to success in playing a string instrument. When a reasonable degree of proficiency is reached in those areas, the cerebral aspects of music study become easier. The student is relieved of the burden of learning both the physical and intellectual simultaneously.

Again, as in the early stages of learning speech, parents' participation is highly recommended to ensure that they are informed on the process at hand and consequently, are capable of supervising home study between lessons. Essentially the child first learns to play by ear as s/he learns speech by ear and then learns the technical aspects, which in effect are the grammar and spelling of music at a later time. The program is highly successful and is being used by millions of students throughout the world.

The Traditional Method

The label "traditional" when applied to music teaching methods refers to those procedures that have been in practice since the first lesson. The leitmotif of the consistency of inconsistency appears once again in the world of music but this time in music education. Traditional has come to mean anything that is not Suzuki. Traditional instrumental music teachers begin by teaching the student to hold an instrument in a proper playing position, some basic bowing techniques, and then introducing music reading. This is generally followed by a notation/performance format where the student learns to play a particular note or set of notes from a printed

exercises, etudes, simple songs, and any other collections of notes are used at the discretion of the teacher to achieve success with the student. Since there is no curriculum, the traditional teacher has the flexibility to use anything that will work.

In spite of the Suzuki record of success, there is an ongoing dispute with traditionalists who take opposing positions on most of the Suzuki teaching methods. The following chart outlines some of the views on each side.

SUZUKI METHOD	TRADITIONAL METHOD
Starts formal training at age 2	Starts formal training age 6-10
Passive observation of others precedes formal study	Immediate note-centered study often one note at a time
Student works with peers sharing common goals and skills	Individualized instruction, single student centered
Assiduously avoids competition	Thrives on competition
Full parent participation	Little to no parent participation
Teaching points guide mastery of technique	Technique pedagogy subject to individual teacher's choice

Summary

Obviously, the rather extensive assortment of pedagogical tools available must work in some way because we have enjoyed instrumental music performance at the highest level for centuries. The question remains as to whom one should choose to activate those tools in a manner that would best suit the needs of a particular student. To find the answer one must engage in a comprehensive investigation of the curriculum vitae of the teachers available along with their record of success and reputation with regard to their student-teacher rapport. On the basis of those findings, one can decide which teacher will most likely be able to succeed with a particular student. When that has been decided, select one, hope for the best, keep a careful eye on how the entire lesson experience is progressing, and if necessary, at some point make a change.

Chapter 11
The Science of Sound

Sound occurs when a force excites vibrations in the atmosphere. These vibrations are projected by a series of compressed and released waves of air pressure. Molecules of air are pushed against one another, acting as a train would when the last car is pushed and each car preceding the last one responds in turn in a chain reaction. Since one single molecule of air cannot travel very far on its own, the molecules must push against one another in order to permit the sound to travel.

When this action and reaction takes place in the air, a wavelike motion produces groupings of molecules positioned in alternating sequences. The first grouping of compressed molecules is referred to as compression. The grouping created by the void left behind the compression is in a more open spatial relationship and is called rarefaction. It is the combined action of compression and rarefaction that results in one complete cycle. (Fig. 11.1)

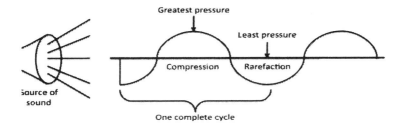

Figure 11.1 Complete Cycle

String Vibration

When vibration is initiated on a string, movement begins at the point of rest or equilibrium (Fig. 11.2, point A). The movement proceeds to its upper limit (point B), begins a return trip traveling back through the original point of rest or equilibrium (point A), and then continues on to the opposite or lower limit (point C). The movement then travels back again returning to the point of equilibrium (point A). This entire voyage completes one cycle. Similarly, one cycle in sound consists of a vibration passing by means of compression and rarefaction through every position which encompasses its point of equilibrium (Fig. 11.2). This type of pure tone is called sinusoidal and its image is called a sine wave.

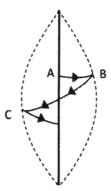

Figure 11.2 Equilibrium

Sine Wave

When sound is generated on a musical instrument, the sound presents itself in a symmetrical pattern of vibrations. These vibrations include a fundamental pitch along with a number of other related pitches sounding in lesser degrees of amplitude or volume. The fundamental pitch alone is a pure tone and can be visualized as a simple wave, free from any accompanying vibrations or tones (Fig. 11.3).

Figure 11.3   Sine Wave

Harmonics

Pure tones are best produced electronically and are generally considered to be musically uninteresting. When a tone is generated on a musical instrument, it is almost always accompanied by a series of related sounds or tones called harmonics, overtones, or upper partials. These three terms can be used interchangeably.

Harmonics (overtones, upper partials) are secondary vibrations occurring concurrently with the fundamental pitch and consist of successive multiples of the whole vibrating body. The segments occur as 1/2, 1/3, 1/4, etc., of the original vibrating column and sound with less amplitude than the fundamental pitch (Fig. 11.4).

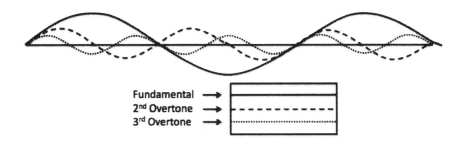

Figure 11.4 Harmonics

Harmonics are embellishments of the pitch. They are not distinguishable by the listener as entities in themselves but rather serve as ornamentation to the fundamental pitch. As such, harmonics give a distinctive character to a pitch, allowing the listener to distinguish among the different instruments or voices.

Hertz

Vibrations per second are commonly referred to as cycles per second (cps) or Hertz (Hz), named after the physicist Heinrich Hertz. The number of Hz refers to a number of complete cycles per second, and so 30 Hz means 30 cycles per second. Any given tone is the product of the number of vibrations or cycles which occur per second, e.g., "A" 440 is that tone

which is produced by a sound generator producing 440 vibrations or cycles per second (Fig. 11.5).

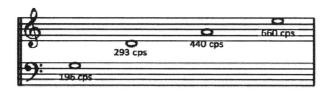

Figure 11.5 Cycles per Second

Although noise is sometimes used in musical performance, tone is more frequently utilized. It is therefore necessary to understand those attributes of sound production which modify noise, thereby converting it into a tone. These attributes are pitch, amplitude and timbre.

Pitch

Pitch refers to the highness or lowness of tone. The notes of an ascending scale (do, re, mi, fa, sol, la, ti, do) go up in pitch or are successively higher (Fig. 11.6). Conversely, in a descending scale (do, ti, la, sol, fa, mi, re, do) the notes go down in pitch or are successively lower (Fig. 11.7).

Figure 11.6 Ascending Scale   **Figure 11.7 Descending Scale**

Any series of notes can take one of only three possible directions in pitch. They can ascend (Fig. 11.8A), descend (Fig. 11.8B), or remain the same (Fig. 11.8C).

Figure 11.8 Directions in Pitch

Amplitude

Amplitude, a form of energy, refers to the volume or loudness of a sound. Greater amplitude produces louder sounds whereas less amplitude produces softer sounds. A sine wave is a way of representing a single frequency with no harmonics. If a sine wave is used to measure the amplitude of a tone, the amplitude is indicated by the distance from the point of equilibrium to the outermost limit of the sine curve (Fig. 11.9).

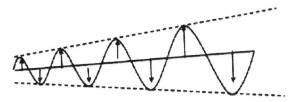

Figure 11.9 Amplitude

As is the case with any force, there is a gradual diminution of the energy as it is confronted with resistance such as friction, absorption, or dispersion. Because of this gradual decline in energy, the tone will dissipate or fade away.

Amplitude (volume) is one of the several physical components that go into the total character of a musical tone. Amplitude is the force with which the sound is being produced and is commonly referred to as volume or loudness. The more forceful the vibrations per second, the louder the sound. Conversely, the weaker the vibrations per second, the softer the sound. Amplitude does not affect pitch. Any pitch can be produced at any amplitude and therefore, can sound at any volume.

Timbre

Timbre is the product of the addition of tones to a fundamental pitch. These additional sounds referred to as harmonics (overtones, or upper partials, see Fig. 11.4) result from the inherent acoustical characteristics of the sound-producing mechanism, i.e., the instrument producing the sound.

For the note, C, these sounds follow the harmonic sequence pictured in Figure 11.10 and are present in most tones. The same interval pattern would occur for any note.

Figure 11.10 Harmonic Sequence

The difference in timbre that is sensed by the listener is the result of the strength (volume/amplitude) of the additional sounds (harmonics), and how they relate in volume to the fundamental pitch. The greater the strength, volume, or amplitude of the additional sounds (harmonics) the more intense the nature or timbre of the sound of the instrument.

The less strength/volume/amplitude of the additional sounds (harmonics), the less intense the timbre. An example is the oboe. Tones played on an oboe have strong harmonics/upper partials producing a tone which can be identified as having an intense timbre. The flute, on the other hand, has a comparatively weak set of harmonics/upper partials and, therefore, produces a more mellow tone.

Summary

Sound occurs when a force excites vibrations in the atmosphere. When a tone is generated on a musical instrument, it is almost always accompanied by a series of related sounds or tones called harmonics, overtones, or upper partials. These secondary vibrations embellish the fundamental pitch giving it a distinctive sound quality or timbre. Pitch refers to the highness or lowness of tone. Amplitude refers to the volume or loudness of a sound.

Appendix

Instrument Diary

This chapter is designed to document the history and maintenance of an instrument. By entering all the relevant information on a regular basis, the owner will have a reference for periodic maintenance, information for a possible sale in the future, and a history of the instrument both past and future. Not every category listed will be relevant to every instrument. Fill in those that are relevant and add any information that suits your particular situation.

My (Instrument) _____

Instrument's History

Owner's name _____

Date of purchase _____

Where purchased _____

Maker's label _____

Model name and number _____

Date made _____

New []   previously owned []

Previous owner(s) name(s)

_____

Identifying marks, label, serial number_____

_____

Seller's Information

Name   _____

Address   _____

Phone   _____

Email   _____

Website   _____

List or asking price   _____

Price paid   _____

Notes

N.B. When making an entry include date, action, repair, replacement or service, part serviced, brand or description of replacement part, source, technician's name and contact information, etc., keep all invoices in a file for future reference.

Maintenance Record

The Instrument – General Service

Date	Service	Cost

String Changes

Date	Service	Cost

Peg

Date	Service	Cost

Nut

Date	Service	Cost

Bridge

Date	Service	Cost

Tailpiece

Date	Service	Cost

Tail Gut

Date	Service	Cost

Fine Tuners

Date	Service	Cost

Saddle

Date	Service	Cost

End Pin or End Button

Date	Service	Cost

Major Repairs

Detail the damage, cause, how repaired, by whom, cost, date.

Date	Service	Cost

Notes

The Bow

Rehair

Date	Service	Cost

Cleaning

Date	Service	Cost

Repair

Date	Service	Cost

Other

Date	Service	Cost

Glossary of Terms

This chapter is designed to help the reader identify items and define terms that are present in the everyday life of a string instrument owner. The glossary defines bowing terms most commonly used and the word/picture dictionary allows the reader to search the meaning of a term either by words in alphabetical order or by recognizing a picture of the subject item.

Terms Used for Bowing Directions

Note: The universal language for music is Italian; however, this does not preclude one using any other language to express musical terms.

Arco (Italian) Use the bow to play this section.

Au Talon (French) Play this passage at the frog end of the bow.

Avec le Bois (French) Use the bow stick in place of the bow hair to bow the string.

Col Legno Battuto (Italian) Strike the string with the wooden bow stick using a bouncing motion.

Collé (French) Use a light but clearly articulated short bow stroke. Attack from above with a brief contact with the string and then a clean release upward.

Col Legno Tratto (Italian) Use the bow stick in place of the bow hair to bow the string.

Détaché (French) Bow individually articulated notes smoothly with no pause between them.

Détaché Lance (French) Bow individually articulated notes smoothly with a slight pause between them. The notes are not separate.

Flautando   (Italian) Direct the bowing pattern closer or slightly over the edge of the fingerboard. This will modify the sound to more closely resemble that of a flute. (See Sul Tasto below.)

Jeté (French) Throw the bow across the string to make it bounce, producing a series of short notes. Similar to skipping a rock across water.

Legato   (Italian) Use a smooth bowing motion with no articulation between notes except for the change in pitch.

Marcato   (Italian) Use a strongly articulated bold stroke.

Martelé   (French) Use an aggressive, accented attack to the note with immediate release.

Martellato   (Italian) Use an aaggressive, accented attack to the note with immediate release.

Pizzicato   (Italian) Pluck the string.

Ponticello   (Italian) Direct the bowing close to the bridge to produce a more aggressive sound. See Sul Ponticello below.

Punta d'arco   (Italian) Direct the bowing to the tip of the bow to produce a less aggressive sound.

Ricochet   (French) Bounce the bow off the string in a succession of notes.

Sautillé   (French) Use a light, resilient bow stroke bouncing across the string.

Spiccato   (Italian) Use a bouncing bow stroke across the string to produce very short separated notes

Staccato   (Italian) Produce a short note using any of the "separated note" techniques listed.

Sul   (Italian) Sul means "On". It is also used to indicate "near" as in "sul pointicello". The Italian word for near is actually vecino.

Sul Pointicello   (Italian) Bow near the bridge to produce a more aggressive sound.

Tasto   (Italian) The fingerboard.

Sul Tasto   (Italian) Bow over or near the fingerboard in order to modify the sound to resemble that of a flute.

Tremolo   (Italian) Play the same note repeatedly by moving the bow back and forth rapidly with a wrist motion.

String Instrument Parts

N.B. This glossary can be used by seeking a term listed in alphabetical order or finding the picture that matches the part in question.

Back   The back of the body of a string instrument. Also referred to as the back plate.

Bass Bar   The bass bar is located on the underside of the top of

the instrument, reinforcing the top while supporting the great force exerted by the tension of the strings. It also distributes the vibrations throughout the top.

Belly   The top of a string instrument. Sometimes called the top plate.

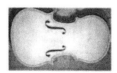

Bib A bib is designed to protect the finish of a double bass from scratches and the wear which can occur as the body of the bass is in contact with the player's body. Bibs contain pockets for small items such as rosin.

Bridge A bridge supports the strings on an instrument and transfers sound from a vibrating string to the body of the instrument.

Bridge Adjuster A bridge adjuster facilitates the raising and lowering a bridge with the turn of a screw.

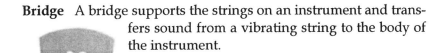

Bow   A bow is a slightly curved staff made of wood or a manmade substance strung with horsehair or fiberglass hair substitute. When used the ribbon of hair is drawn across the strings of the instrument to produce sound.

Bow Hair   Horse hair or a man-made substitute is strung across a bow and serves as the point of contact with the string as the instrument is played.

Bow Quiver   An oblong case usually made of leather designed to hold double bass bows conveniently and safely. Can be used for all other bows.

Body   The name given to the main part of a string instrument. The body (front, back and sides) amplifies the sound produced by the vibrating strings.

Block   A wooden block placed at key points in the structure of a string instrument to strengthen the unit. One block is placed in each corner where the upper and lower bouts meet the C bout. One block is placed at the bottom of the body to reinforce the end pin and one block placed at the top of the body to reinforce the neck contact.

Bout The term used to identify the three sections of the body. The upper third is called the upper bout, the mid- section is called the C bout, and the lower third is called the lower bout.

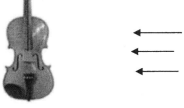

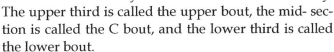

Chin Rest An appliance designed to provide a comfortable and secure placement of a player's chin when one holds a violin or viola in playing position. Chin rests are available in a wide variety of configurations to accommodate the endless variation of the human chin to shoulder relationship.

End Button A wooden wedge-shaped piece inserted in the end of a violin or viola on which a tail gut is hooked to hold the tailpiece in place.

End Pin An adjustable rod extending from the bottom of a cello or double bass. The rod can be adjusted to permit the player to raise or lower the instrument to a comfortable playing position.

Electronic Tuner   This mechanism provides a pitch, a series of pitches, and/or a visual illustration of the accuracy of a pitch for tuning purposes.

"F" Hole   Sometimes called a sound hole, a decorative aperture resembling the shape of the letter "f" serving as an escape for the sound vibrations which occur when a string instrument is being played.

Fine Tuner   A device designed to facilitate the tuning of a string to the very slightest degree. Various iterations allow placement on a string, on a tailpiece, or built into a tailpiece.

Fingerboard   A part of all string instruments, this hardwood board (usually ebony), extends from the peg box to provide a surface against which the player can press the string to change pitches.

Lining   Thin strips of wood glued around the inside edge of the ribs of an instrument to act as a support.

Machine Head A gear system in place of the wedge shaped pegs used on the violin, viola, and cello. This system is designed to support the higher tension of tuned double bass strings.

Mute A mute lessens the vibrations traveling from a string through the bridge of an instrument in order to alter the tone quality and volume of the sound.

Pickup A microphone or electromagnetic contact device that transmits the vibrations from a string instrument to an amplifier and speaker setup. The three types illustrated are piezoelectric, omnidirectional, and bimorphic.

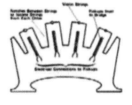

Peg   A wedge-shaped piece of wood used to tune strings on a string instrument. The string is inserted into a hole in the peg and as the peg is turned, the string winds up and is tightened.

Piezoelectric Pickup   A form of electronic pickup used to amplify musical instruments. (See pickup.)

Purfling   Two parallel strips of hard wood, usually ebony, inlaid into the surface around the edge of the top and back of an instrument. The groove cut for the inlay acts as an interruption for the vibrations which travel through the wood while strengthening the edges of the instrument.

Rib   The sides of a string instrument.

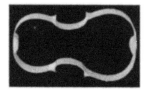

Saddle a hardwood bar placed at the end of the top plate to support the tail gut and prevent damage to the body.

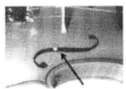

Sound Post A wooden dowel acting as a structural support for the top of the instrument. A sound post, made of soft wood, conducts the vibrations produced by the higher strings from the top of the instrument to its back while muting any echo effect which would occur if that post were not present.

Scroll The decorative top of a string instrument.

Scroll Eye The center of a scroll.

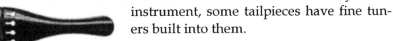

Tailpiece A device to which the lower end of the strings on an instrument are attached. Located at the bottom of the body of the instrument, some tailpieces have fine tuners built into them.

Tailgut   A short piece of gut or nylon that secures the tailpiece to the end button.

Wolf Tone Eliminator   A device applied to a string to eliminate a sound (wolf tone) which can occur on some instruments where a particular note will match the natural frequency of that instrument.

Index

About the Author

Michael Pagliaro has served as professor of instrumental music and musical instrument technology, is founder and CEO emeritus-in-counsel of Ardsley Musical Instrument Service, Ltd., and director of research and development for Contemporary Music Laboratories. He is an authority in musical instrument technology and the inventor of several musical instrument products. He is author of *Everything You Should Know about Musical Instruments* (1992), *The Violin: How It Works* (2002), *The Flute: How It Works* (2003), *The Violin Workbook* (2004), *The Musical Instrument Desk Reference* (Scarecrow Press, 2012), *and The Instrumental Music Director's Guide to Comprehensive Program Development* (Rowman and Littlefield, 2014).